Penguin Books
Rites, Black and White

Robert Brain was born in Tasmania in 1933. He attended
the University of Tasmania and London University as an
anthropology student, and then was a lecturer from 1960
to 1969. He has written academic books based on his
anthropological studies in Cameroun and Mali in West
Africa. In addition, he has published a novel and several
general books about different societies and cultures,
including *Love and Friendship* which has appeared in
English, French and German.

He lives in Italy and earns his living from writing and
translating.

Robert Brain

Rites, Black and White

Penguin Books

Penguin Books Ltd,
Harmondsworth, Middlesex, England
Penguin Books,
625 Madison Avenue, New York, N.Y. 10022, U.S.A.
Penguin Books Australia Ltd,
Ringwood, Victoria, Australia
Penguin Books Canada Ltd,
2801 John Street, Markham, Ontario, Canada
Penguin Books (N.Z.) Ltd,
182-190 Wairau Road, Auckland 10, New Zealand

First published by Penguin Books Australia 1979

Made and printed in Australia at
The Dominion Press, North Blackburn, Victoria
Set in Palatino by The Dova Type Shop, Melbourne

Brain, Robert.
Rites, black and white.

ISBN 0 14 070078 1

1. Rites and ceremonies. I. Title.

301.21

Contents

Preface

This is a book of ideas. Hence the facts must be brief. The usual estimate for the population of Black Australians at the time of their first contact with European settlers is three hundred thousand. Population densities were much higher in the coastal fertile areas where 90 per cent of fourteen million White Australians now live, greatly outnumbering their Black brothers. The nomadic Black Australian survived longest in north-western South Australia, the middle-eastern part of Western Australia and the central-western region of the Northern Territory where tribal territories were large but food was never concentrated or plentiful. A study of the tribes of this area – the Aranda, the Pidjandjadjara, Dieri, Walbiri and Wuradjeri – provides most of the material for this book.

Finally, one or two slightly apologetic explanations. Firstly, throughout this book I have used what is known as the ethnographic present. The people I call Black Australians and talk about in the present tense have lost their original culture. Fifty years ago half of the Black population of Australia was nomadic, living a traditional way of life; today, there are no completely nomadic Black Australians left. Since the beginning of colonial conquest, the Blacks have been relegated to more and more arid areas, pushed aside by White expansion; their animals have been hunted, their women kidnapped, their children sent to White schools and their manpower co-opted by the Whites. In robbing the Blacks of their land and parting them from their physical resources, the Whites have also wrecked their spiritual past, present and future. Few Black Australians perform their rites and ceremonies any more, or recite the myths and legends, so that most of the material in this book refers to twenty, fifty, even a hundred years ago. In fact, it is probably true to say that the fully nomadic culture of the Black Australians was destroyed by the end of the nineteenth century, so that no modern anthropologist has ever been able to present a picture of fully functioning 'Black life as it was'. I have used material from the early 1800s to the 1970s, culling details concerned with passage rites from all the available sources and presenting them in the present tense *as if* they were fully functioning. This is a standard anthropological practice and avoids the confusion of continual tense jumping and dating. The same holds for accounts of Australian life: although my own personal experiences of infancy, puberty and early adolescence happened thirty years ago, I have described them in the present tense, and have interspersed contemporary anecdotes among them.

Secondly, I have used the bold, blanket terms Black and White Australians to describe two populations which have a greater degree of physical and cultural variation than these terms may suggest. How can I justify lumping five hundred tribes with different cultural traditions and different territories under the general name of Black Australians? I am aware that some groups don't throw boomerangs; that only in Arnhem Land is the didjeridoo found; that some people incise churinga stones while others paint coloured ritual patterns on the ground or on bark. I am aware that the Black Australians inhabited environments from the cool-temperate one in the south, through the arid zone in the centre to the tropical area in the north and north-east. I am aware that Black Australians had no lingua franca – no language understood from one end of the continent to the other. I am aware that one tribe reckons descent exclusively through the father, some of its neighbours through the mother and others through both; that is, in anthropological terms, there were patrilineal and matrilineal groups, and others had double descent.

Yet, the homogeneity of both Black and White groups overrides their heterogeneity; in no other continent have two groups living side by side each exhibited such a striking degree of homogeneity. Prior to the Second World War, White Australians were probably the most uniform nation in the world: from Cape York to Hobart in Tasmania it was possible to define a particular White Australian style of speech, a common set of values in the towns, the cities and the countryside. It is only during the last thirty years that the predominantly British character of the White Australian population has been radically changed with the addition of large numbers of immigrants from central and southern Europe.

Black Australians, in a superficial sense, are much less homogeneous than the antipodean representatives of the western world, of a civilization founded on Greece, the Renaissance, Christianity and Capitalism. Nevertheless, it is generally agreed that Black Australians are remarkably uniform in culture and physical characteristics (contact with outsiders to the north explains occasional variations in physical appearance). All Black Australians lived the hunting life; all used stone implements such as stone-headed axes and scrapers; all used spears and clubs and throwing-sticks; all made some kind of wind-break and wet-weather shelter; all made fire by friction and cooked food in the fire or earthovens of hot stones; all were divided into clans and sections. They had no money; they had strong food taboos; most went without clothes; none made intoxicating drinks; and they performed passage rites with the same basic symbolism and ritual procedure.

I should also point out to non-Australians who are used to calling a spade a spade that it is unusual in Australia to call the original Australians 'Blacks'; they have always been known as 'Aborigines', although today 'Aboriginals' is considered more becoming. To write about 'Blacks and Whites' suggests to official Australia the kind of racial confrontation that intellectuals and bureaucrats have tried to avoid. Yet, Black and White are convenient words with definite physical and cultural meanings and both groups have always thought in these terms. Black Australians have always had terms for their colonizers which refer to the shocking colour of their skin and the racist nature of their culture. The term 'Black' is now used in most Black Australian languages to apply to all descendants of the original inhabitants of Australia, even if their blood is much diluted by White Australian blood; it also includes American Negroes and Melanesians. Moreover, Black Australians assume that Blacks were the native peoples of the whole world, and find it hard to believe that England and the rest of Europe were not once occupied by Black people who were ousted by invasive Whites.

Finally, I should like to express my thanks to those informants who talked to me about small-town Australian life and to those hundreds of writers, historians and anthropologists whose work I have plundered to write this highly generalized account of White and Black customs and attitudes. My own work as a social anthropologist has been carried out in Africa, and I am well aware of the dangers in writing a comparative, non-specialized work of this kind. I hope the merit of its ideas will outweigh the inevitable lapses of pure fact. I must also thank Carla Taines for her editorial help.

Robert Brain
January 1979
Batignano, Italy

Introduction

In *Rites, Black and White* I have made a comparison of western and non-western culture patterns in the convinced belief that the differences between Us and Them, between the so-called civilized and primitive, are more apparent than real. I have looked closely at symbolic behaviour in times of crisis, those basic and irreversible moments in life common to human beings everywhere, whether we inhabit a Sydney garden-suburb or the central Australian desert, whether the savage wears a twin-set or a coat of feathers and paint. In all societies, ceremony and rite embellish the biological rhythms of our existence through birth, weaning, puberty, marriage, parenthood, old age to death.

I am a Tasmanian and an anthropologist, certainly an ironic combination: I am the descendant of White Australians who exterminated a unique people within a couple of generations. My childhood in the 1930s and 1940s was spent on an island uncontaminated by Blacks although our teachers and parents regularly took us to the local museum to look at the stone tools and rock engravings of the original Tasmanians. We trailed morosely around dark dank rooms looking at marsupials and human bones and human hair. One of the best-known fetish objects of the White Tasmanians was the articulated skeleton of 'Queen Victoria' or Truganini, the last of the Tasmanian race.

At school we wrote essays about Black Tasmanians. I remember writing mostly about what they did *not* have: no clothes, no knowledge of fire making, no dogs and cats, no farms, no houses, no pots and pans, no baskets, no means of boiling water, no religion only a primitive system of magic and sorcery. Strange vested interests seemed to want to portray Black Tasmanians as simple, child-like folk, children of instinct and nature. Before the Second World War all the available literature on Black Tasmanians and Black Australians described them as lazy food gatherers and helpless children. They lay around in the sun or huddled together against the rain, occasionally picking up a boomerang to throw at a kangaroo, squandering their energies on 'corroborees', brawling, mutilating their bodies or beating their women. Sensible observers felt they had to apologize for the sexuality, the nakedness, the cruelty of the Black Australians. Even anthropologists adopted paternalistic attitudes. Berndt writes 'Our children feel very much at the mercy of a world they do not yet understand and they accept readily the conception of fairies, gnomes, witches and giants. Nomadic Aborigines are at much that level of sophistication.' Consequently, we little White Tasmanians felt compassion for the dead Black Tasmanians and vaguely understood that they were hardly worthy of survival; all was for the best in the best of all possible white worlds, although we knew that on the Australian mainland the Wild Ones still stalked the deserts of Arnhem Land and the slums of Sydney.

I grew up, left Tasmania, and, by-passing the Australian continent, spent many years in Europe and Africa adapting to strange new cultures: Norfolk, England; Leopoldville, Congo; Grosseto, Italy; Bangwa, Cameroon. Far away from Australia I learned that it was a quite unjustified assumption that pure reason, morals and the good life were prerogatives of white civilization, while the world of unreason and evil and savagery was inhabited by the black, brown, and yellow races. I learned that there were many different 'right' ways of growing up, making a living, believing in god, greeting neighbours. I came back to Tasmania in 1977 with the knowledge that human beings throughout the world share similar basic needs, but satisfy them in different exotic ways. I realized that the extinct Black Tasmanians must have had a complex culture, a religion and a developed moral sense, even though my ancestors had not bothered to study their myths, their cosmology, their ways of thought. After spending twenty years trying to understand and adapt to different cultures, and surviving some major and minor culture shocks, I wanted to come to terms with Black Australians and wipe out those years standing mute and stupid in front of Truganini's bones.

Like most Australians my knowledge of Black Australians came from books. Studying anthropology in Great Britain I discovered to my amazement that the poor Aborigine I had learned about in whimsical radio serials and children's books had a renowned international reputation. Freud used the sexual symbolism of their initiation rites to develop his theories of the subconscious and his explanation of Oedipal fantasies of primordial lust, murder, guilt and fears of castration. Robertson-Smith wrote on Black Australian 'sacrificial totemic feasts'; Sir James Frazer filled volumes of *The Golden Bough* with theories based on Black Australian ideas of the 'external soul'; the French sociologist, Durkheim, derived his ideas of the 'totemic principle' from Australian ethnography; recently Lévi-Strauss has enlivened drawing-rooms and academic sanctuaries of Europe and America with his theories of the universality of the human mind again using Black Australian myths, totemism and kinship organization.

Aside from their importance in the development of social theory, Black Australians became known in books written by government historians and missionaries and later, travellers and anthropologists. In all of these books, even recent ones, there is a patronizing, 'not-quite-like-us' flavour in the attitudes and even in the language used. In the nineteenth century the Black Australian was described as a 'blackfellow' who lived in 'mobs', had a promiscuous attitude to sex with his 'lubra', had no marriage and committed unspeakable acts during his bloody initiations. Even today, anthropologists write about 'males' instead of men, 'maidens' instead of girls, 'dialects' instead of languages, 'offspring' instead of children. The simple communities of a couple of dozen hunters are called 'hordes' and larger groups are known as 'tribes', words with a derogatory implication, words that suggest wildness and tumultuous aggression – like Tartar 'hordes' or the 'tribes' of Argentinian ants. Even the scientific word 'nomad' has a vaguely disquieting connotation to conservative, settled people who have always felt threatened by nomads as they have felt threatened by yellow hordes; swagmen and gypsies, fossickers and hawkers, surfers and hippies are uprooted people whose very existence disturbs the settled minds of the suburbanites. All these special terms reflect the White's conscious or unconscious superiority, a superiority which once justified abominable acts of cruelty and extermination. Such terms reveal his belief that he is a representative of a western civilization endowed with moral sophistication and high intelligence.

The religions of other peoples – and religion is the main theme of this book – have often been described in very patronizing terms. Although White Australians have a god and even pagan Greeks were permitted gods, Black Australians, at the most, have 'spirits' or 'divinities'. Even anthropologists refuse to use the word 'religion' when discussing the system of beliefs of the Blacks. White Australians have churches and hymns and a creation myth, while Blacks have 'sacred grounds', 'sacred songs' and the 'dreaming'. Both Black and White cultures have sacraments but those of the Blacks are called 'magical rites'.

Because they are not christians, Black Australians are pagans and it is assumed they are also cannibals. 'Pagans and cannibals': the words go together like peaches and cream, white tie and tails. These kinds of beliefs, held strongly by superior-feeling people all over the world, were fanned by early observers of Black Australians who persistently asked to hear stories about cannibalism, seeking a kind of exciting digestive pornography. They were usually obliged. Thus, one early anthropologist wrote, 'As usual, it is by no means easy to find out exactly what takes place, as the natives of the country will assure you that they do not indulge in the habit, but that they know that those of other parts do. When the accused are questioned they, in turn, lay the same charge against their accusers and so on, often from group to group.' Every seasoned anthropologist will recognize this situation: the mother-fuckers, the cannibals and the cretins always live on the other side of the river or the mountain; it is an international means of setting Us, the civilized, against Them, the primitive. In fact, no Black Australians have been shown to be genuine cannibals who killed people in order to eat them. If they have eaten human flesh, they ate it for ritual purposes, not because they were hungry or had a fancy for a portion of 'long pig'. Even if they are starving, unlike westerners, they will not eat human flesh; those who die are never eaten by the survivors.

Black and White ritual cannibalism has the same function: it is done to absorb some of the powers of the dead person. Transubstantiation, the marvellous magical change of bread and wine into the blood and flesh of Jesus Christ, does just this. Verily, verily, I say unto you, if you do not eat the flesh of the son of man and drink his blood, ye shall not have life in you.' But Black Australians are not fascinated by the idea of cannibalism as Whites are: we watch films showing people eating people who were even killed for their caloric value, and blood is shown in bucketsful. Swift's cheerful account of Irish women having babies to sell to the rich man's table or the sensational accounts of human meat-eating after aircraft disasters might well persuade an objective anthropologist from outer space to classify Anglo-Saxons as cannibals.

Black Australians, according to White Australians, are not only pagans and cannibals: they are *stupid* pagan cannibals. White Australians have always maintained that the original inhabitants could not think logically or in general and abstract terms. The view is backed up by examples, usually false. Thus it is said that Black Australians have many words for individual trees, fish, snakes and birds, but no abstract terms for 'tree', or 'fish' or 'bird'; that Black Australians believe in magic, in the miraculous increase of animals and totemic spirits; that Black Australians are colour-blind because they have names for red, yellows and white and black only. But are White Australians any more rational and scientific? White Australians, for example, are 'smell-blind' – they recognize countless different smells, but have never given them names. The number of named smells or colours simply depends on the way the colour or the smell spectrum is divided up by a particular society. White Australians who happen to be christians believe that Jesus Christ is the 'son of man', the 'son of god' and the product of virgin birth. They do not consider themselves illogical, yet it is clear that such ideas are no more rational and scientific than Pidjandjadjara totemic beliefs. Moreover, while a Black Australian can explain most of his equipment, technical and cosmological, Whites often simply take their culture for granted. Most of us are unsure of the exact nature of our religious beliefs and a few people, like my Aunt Daisy, think that the sun goes round the earth and that a videotape, or even a firework, functions as if by magic. Black Australians and White Australians act along different lines and may even think along different lines, but each group thinks logically given the assumptions of its basic symbolic system.

Not only do small-town White Australians, who view 'darkies' and 'abos' as benighted creatures of the wild, believe in the illogicality of Black Australians, but some intellectuals, even those with university qualifications, find the mind of the Black Australian simply ungraspable. Let me look at a simple example from a recent history about Black Australians by Blainey. Some Black Australians (including the dead Tasmanians) refuse to eat scaled fish, but they have no taboo against eating dog meat. This historian, mistakenly, looks for a rational reason for this taboo on fish; yet, it would not occur to him to look for a rational reason why White Australians eat scaled fish, but do not eat dogs. Blainey writes that 'The Tasmanian taboo on fish other than shellfish cannot be explained in terms of medical knowledge', using what I call the 'hygienic theory' to justify human behaviour. This 'hygienic theory' is used to explain why jews do not eat pig or why most human beings do not sleep with their mothers: because it is bad for the stomach or the race. Blainey suggests that Tasmanians once ate fish which had rotted and having become ill, never ate any fish again: for two thousand years, memory of rotten fish deprived the Tasmanians of one of their most abundant and nutritious foods. We must certainly have a poor idea of the mentality of people with scaled-fish and pork taboos, if we really imagine they derive from motives of hygiene.

With a little thought, and a quick comparison with similar taboos in our own culture, we soon realize that people do not refuse to eat animals because they 'go off' or because of their dirty habits. White Australians gobble up the oysters that grow in the filth and excrement of Sydney harbour: they go bad quickly, they have dirty habits and they are eaten alive. Oysters are known to make people sick and can be carriers of typhoid and cholera, but we have not bothered to taboo them. Food is selected as tabooed food for symbolic reasons. As Lévi-Strauss neatly points out, some food prescriptions – eating fish on Fridays, for example – occur not because the food is 'good to eat', but because it is 'good to think'; the food is part of a pattern of thought. And as for proscriptions: scaled fish were proscribed to the illogical Tasmanians in the same way as dog is proscribed to illogical White Australians. In a few hundred years, an archaeologist will discover that White Australians never ate dog, while their Chinese neighbours did. He would be foolish to suggest that such a rich source of protein was tabooed because the Australians had once had an upset stomach after eating bad stewed leg of dog. Although he might not know that the White Australian's dog was 'man's best friend', he will have to assume that the taboo, like the jews' taboo on pork, is a symbolic act, not merely a rule of hygiene.

Today attitudes towards Black Australians are changing. Like the U.S. government, that in the 1930s changed its relations with the Indians, Australian administrators with the support of the intelligentsia have decided, a little late, that Black culture will be allowed to survive. White Australians, surveying their own cultural desert, are beginning to look with envy at the dramatic symbol-ridden world they destroyed. At universities the languages of extinct tribes are being taught to enthusiastic Whites, and artists, writers and composers are turning to the remnants of Black culture for inspiration. Inevitably Black civilization has been romanticized and bowdlerized: Black myths, rituals and art have been turned into children's stories, meaningless ballets and ashtrays. Like Americans who idealize Indian culture, White Australians are hanging Aboriginal sacred objects next to their Impressionist paintings and they visit Ayer's Rock in the comfort of air-conditioned buses and buy toy boomerangs from the disinherited Blacks.

Attitudes are less 'enlightened' in the small towns and suburbs of Australia where Aboriginals are still thought of as 'dirty' and 'infantile', with strong sexual and weak moral instincts. It seems ridiculous to have to insist that Black Australians live in families and do not eat their children; that 8 or 10 or 15 per cent of both Black and White Australians are left-handed or homosexual; that there are Black and White psychotics, adulterers, masturbators, suicides. Black and White Australians have similar sexual appetites, similar aggressive natures, similar loving attitudes and live in ordered communities under systems of law, society and morality. Black Australians are not 'primitive people' but human beings living primitively; White Australians are not 'civilized people', but people living with the potential advantages of three thousand years of western civilization.

According to many White Australians, there is only one Right Way – the Christian, Civilized Way: all others are pagan, primitive and wrong. Yet, in reality our methods of making love, giving birth, growing up, even eating and shitting are matters of faith and dogma. I remember my own young, shocked sense of disbelief when I found that all people do not adopt the missionary position for sex, do not stand (for men) or squat (for women) when urinating, sit when defecating or awkwardly lie down when giving birth. These ethnocentric attitudes help produce the disastrous conservatism that vehemently resists change; such a mentality defends everything in suburbia as 'best' and 'normal', and everything else is viewed as 'worst' and 'abnormal' – a prejudiced monster image that lumps all blacks, communists, foreigners and freaks together.

The great variety of greeting behaviours show the differences in symbolic meaning from society to society. When I left Australia at the age of twenty I knew that men greet one another with a cursory nod, a quick thump on the back or a brief 'hello'; kissing and other close body contact is the preserve of women and children. Once out of Australia, I had to re-learn day-to-day etiquette. In Italy, I shook hands continually and learned the formal greetings for different kinds of people and different times of day. In Africa, I did not shake hands with my friends, but imitated their endless greetings which reflected a person's activity – whether he was getting up, walking towards the forest, sitting, standing or eating – rather than his status.

When I returned to Tasmania, I unlearned many habits I had picked up in Europe. I stopped shaking hands and I kissed only small children and elderly aunts; I made very few mistakes because I had learned the culture as a child. I came back to Tasmania with an Italian who was joining his family – a Tasmanian wife and three children – after an absence of many years. His natural inclination was to kiss them all, all the time. His eighteen-year-old son, a real Australian now, took me aside and asked me to explain to his father that grown men in Australia do not kiss: it is considered effeminate and vaguely primitive.

This situation jogged my memory and I thought about the Black Tasmanians when they first saw White men, the Dutch, French and English explorers in the seventeenth and eighteenth centuries. At each meeting the Tasmanians showed great friendliness to the peculiar, white-skinned men with their wrapped-up legs, who arrived in floating islands and who had sticks that exploded and killed without any visible force. Cook wrote that the Tasmanians welcomed his men with 'benevolent expressions' and 'quick sparkling eyes' and they brought the strangers fresh meat and water. These sailors would have seemed much weirder to the Tasmanians than martian invaders would seem to us. At least we now have an idea that people may exist on another planet, while the Black Tasmanians probably thought the world and the universe belonged to them.

How did the Black Tasmanians greet their guests? Peron, the French naturalist, was met by Black Tasmanians on the shore waving their spears and stamping their feet. He was not aware that the Tasmanians were expressing their friendly feelings by wildly stamping their feet and he ordered his men to approach the gesticulating men and to kiss them. To Peron's amazement, the Tasmanians repulsed their oral advances with as much embarrassment as the eighteen-year-old Italo-Tasmanian. Peron wrote in his diary that the civilized custom of kissing seemed, strange to say, unknown to the Tasmanians but that he would try again the next day to teach the savages.

Peron, ethnocentrically, imagined that the kiss, rather than the stamping of feet or the rubbing of noses, was the universal sign of goodwill. White Australian men have a 'healthy' aversion to it and to most tender physical touching. Black Tasmanians, who had never heard of kissing – the joining of the entrances of the digestive tract – might have considered it rather unhygienic and unattractive, suggestive of the eating habits of the snake which moistens its victim with saliva before swallowing it. The Black Tasmanians might have thought that the cannibal Whites were tasting them; or that they were feeding them, as only when babies or very old people were fed with premasticated food did Blacks touch mouth to mouth.

On the mainland, Black Australian greeting etiquette is different again. In one group, they neither stamp their feet nor kiss: they perform the penis-holding ceremony. When a Black Australian visitor arrives for a ceremony he approaches in turn each of the seated hosts who lifts his arm. He presses his penis against his host's hand, so that the subincised urethra is in full contact with the palm, and then draws the penis along his hand. Penis-holding is a symbolic sign of friendship in exactly the same way as kissing, foot-stamping or rubbing noses. If the contact is refused, friendship has been refused and fighting may follow. Oddly enough, while Peron and Cook might have been startled by the penis-holding ceremony, White Australians today may find it less unusual than men kissing: in horseplay between mates, grabbing each other's genitals is considered quite a friendly masculine gesture.

I began my field work in Tasmania, turning my porno-voyeurist eyes on my friends and relatives, neighbours and strangers with the same bold attitude I had adopted in African villages where I was never afraid to ask the most intimate question about the most intimate behaviour. I went into living rooms, bedrooms and toilets; I attended games and ceremonies; I gained entrance to private clubs; I spied on family rites. I tried to needle out the hidden meanings of body taboos, attitudes to menstruation, pubic hair, pierced ears. Social anthropologists have theorized happily about circumcision in primitive society, but few have discussed penis mutilation or vaginal cuts in our own society. Like Jesus Christ, whose mother carried his foreskin around with her for many years, thousands of White Australians are circumcised so I tried to find out why. Instead of travelling the bush in a khaki safari suit, armed with flyspray and water filter, discussing pregnancy taboos, ritual sodomy, vagina envy among the Blacks, I asked similar questions in the suburbs.

I found the going hard. My prying was often misunderstood. Sitting in an African hut or by an Australian waterhole, the White anthropologist with his notebook, his bonhomie, his patient understanding, his Landrover and his gentle bribes of money, tobacco or drink, is bolstered by his hidden power as a representative of a superior civilization. Sometimes he is accompanied by government officers as well as gifts. In this way it is easy to persuade informants to reveal the secrets of their sexual life, their family organization, even their sacred rites. But the anthropologist who asks the White inhabitants of a small Tasmanian town about their attitudes to incest and the menopause, anal symbolism and homoeroticism is marked as a dirty old man rather than an objective scientist.

I persevered, attending ceremonies, going to parties, drinking and eating with the natives. I attended their corroborees. One of these was a gymkhana in a small Victorian town. I watched the horse racing; I guessed the weight of a mighty ewe; I took part in the drive-in-the-nail competition and I ducked my head in a bucket of water trying to pick up an orange in my mouth. Anthropologists call this 'participant observation'. I joined the crowd of men around the busy bar and kept away from the tent where the local ladies were making and having afternoon-tea. Towards the end of the afternoon, I watched the young farmers playing a violent game of musical chairs with motor cars and two local groups

engaged in a ferocious tug-of-war. When my friends asked
me what I thought of their gymkhana, I said it was great;
it reminded me of an African ceremony. They laughed when
I suggested that cars and beer were symbols of the men's
world, cakes and tea of the women's. I made the anthropologist's usual remarks about the phallic symbolism of the
drive-in-the-nail game; the totemic significance of the ewe;
the role of the feud and moiety organization in the tug-of-war
between two neighbouring villages; the significance of the
oval, egg-shaped, sacred ground. Yes, it was very nice, very
primitive, I said. The others laughed and asked where the
gory initiation mutilations, the tree worship, the orgies were.

Just as I thought it was all over, a cheerful woman came
around with a basket of eggs donated by the Victorian Egg
Board. All the women took one and formed a line across
the oval ground, while the men, looking vaguely embarrassed, lined up opposite them. One woman's husband had
been called away, so I found myself ten yards away from
a farmer's buxom wife who was aiming an egg at me. The
women threw: some of the eggs fell to the ground; others
hit the husbands squarely in the chest or face and broke in
a slimy mess; most of them were caught and lobbed back
to wives or fiancées. At each throw, the lines were sent
further apart so that after a hilarious half-hour, only two
couples were left quietly throwing seemingly unbreakable
eggs at each other from a distance of about a hundred yards.
The rest of us stood around, strangely exhilarated, cleaning
eggs from our faces and clothes until the last couple broke
their egg. I told my friends that the ceremony had all the
elements of a typical fertility ritual: eggs, the sacred ground,
men and women the ritual of rebellion when down-trodden
women threw things at their husbands. Only the feast and
sexual licence were lacking. Again they looked at me,
laughed good-naturedly, then drove off in their Landrovers,
panel vans and station wagons to drink at the hotel and dance
with the girls through the night.

Sunday morning, the fire-bell rang and I found myself
involved in my first serious bushfire. I went with another
'townie' and half-heartedly sprayed the flickering flames

while fire trucks roared up the bracken-covered slopes of the valley crowded with boys, youths, men: the farmers of yesterday's gymkhana. They fought the fire with hoses, sandbags, brush-brooms, even bulldozers and an aeroplane. They beat back the flames with gusto, clothes scorched by the heat, hair singed, faces blackened by smoke; they were happy in mateship and danger, dreaming of protecting old Australian homesteads where the women, in neat print frocks, made tea, sandwiches and chocolate cakes. By evening, the fire was out and the men, black and blear-eyed, retired to the local hotel with an honest excuse to drink a few extra gallons of beer and talk over the excitement of the day: how close the fire had got to old Bill's stables and to the state forest of 'penis radiator'. We all decided that the fire had been started by a couple of hitch-hikers, who had been camping down by Rudge's Creek.

Bushfires, hitch-hikers, chocolate cakes and ale. What do these things have to do with the Black nomads wiped out of the area a hundred years ago? One of the unwarranted prejudices of White Australians is that Black Australians were childish firebugs who burned miles of bush for the hell of it or just to catch a couple of meagre wallaby rats. The White Australians who destroyed mighty eucalyptuses by ring-barking the trees – cutting their life line, the bark, and burning the grey ghost-trees – confined Black Australians to reserves. The farmers feared that these violent despoilers of nature would have burned the sheep farmers off the continent had they not been locked up. As a child, I was shown stretches of button-grass prairies which our schoolteachers told us had once been mighty forests that were burned down by wanton Blacks. It was only years later that I learned that to hunters and gatherers fire had a constructive, not a destructive, meaning. The button-grass plains in Tasmania and the Darling Downs of New South Wales are the result of careful burning off by Black Australians so that fresh pasture for their main source of livelihood, the kangaroo, would grow. When the Whites came these plains were found to be perfect sheep country, and the kangaroo and the Black Australian had to go.

In the Victorian hotel, I listened to the brave firefighters, admiring their rough sense of humour, their generosity on behalf of the local farmers, their frank delight in beer and in the excitement engendered by the bushfire. They talked only about this week's fire, last week's fire, next week's possible fire. Some young farmers seemed to spend all their free time looking for fires to fight. One old man said with a wink that all the best fires happened on dead Sundays. I imagined they broke out on Sundays because the hitch-hikers and campers were around and said so. He said 'Don't be a bloody fool; the police know very well that 80 per cent of the people caught starting fires in Victoria are members of the local fire-brigade.'

Fires started by farmers? Who would believe this after the dramatic television programmes showing miles and miles of pasture-lands burnt out by bushfires, gutted homesteads, stock burnt alive? It is well established that Black Australians have mystical attitudes to fire: they build bonfires during initiation rites, the women throw flaming boughs at the heads of the young men; circumcised initiates stare for hours at the fierce light until they are dazed, half-hypnotized; the wound of the circumcised penis is healed by fire, initiates urinate on the flames, holding their penis above the embers; young Blacks thrust firesticks up their anuses or between their buttocks, then set them alight to see who can leave them there the longest. Fire for the Blacks has a symbolic meaning: it leaves a great impression on young initiates; fire ceremonies are ordeals, acts of purification, and have a cathartic function.

The attitudes of Black Australians to fire have been explained by anthropologists and psychologists in sexual, phallic terms. Freudians maintain that a basic desire of men (not women) is to extinguish fires by peeing on them; setting and extinguishing fires are phallic pleasures for men, who universally associate fires – starting fires, poking fires, putting out fires – with copulation. Freudians add that in growing up, a man loses this infantile desire to start fires and put them out by urinating on them; it has even been suggested that Black Australians subincise the penis – slit it lengthwise on the lower side – to make it ineffective in putting out the precious fire.

White Australians also have irrational attitudes to fire, although the symbolism of the flickering hearth of the Victorian farmsteads has now been replaced by the flickering of the television. I saw White Australians urinating with glee on the burnt-out edges of the bushfire, playing with burning firebrands, taking peculiar pleasure in fire, particularly when it was out of control. Young boys too love starting fires and putting them out by urinating on them: pissing high and long and putting out fires are aspects of White adolescent virility games. 'I want to be a fireman when I grow up' is a common ambition for White boys, and 'hose' is a common slang term for penis. Membership in a fire-brigade allows the youthful excitement associated with fires to continue, but the firefighter uses a real hose instead of a penis.

Black Australian institutions have been interpreted and re-interpreted by anthropologists, while the symbolic activities of White Australians living in the bush, the town and the city, have not. Yet, the behaviour and modes of thought of White Australians in no way exonerate them from the type of analysis carried out on their Black predecessors. The White farmers' thought patterns are equally subjective and primitive, even if they consider their attitudes to the sun and the seasons, puberty and menstruation rational and logical.

Black Australians and White Australians struggle through life on the same vast continent, coping in very different ways with similar problems: bringing up children, teaching them to walk and talk and keep themselves clean; learning about sex, its taboos, marriage; coping with the menopause and death. The ceremonies which accompany these universal steps from the cradle to the grave are known in anthropology as *rites de passage* or passage rites. Black Australians regularly celebrate these crises with ceremonies that symbolize social and physical transformations. Similar radical changes of status – from child to adolescent, from adolescent to adult – are often individual affairs for White Australians.

Arnold van Gennep, a French sociologist, was the first to

call attention to the universal importance of the rites accompanying life crises such as birth, marriage and death. He noted that these events were universally seen as a transition from one status to another: unmarried to married, alive to dead, wife to widow. There is a shift of role: at the birth of their child, married people become parents, at her menarche a girl becomes nubile. In all these passage rites, there are usually three distinct phases: separation, transition and reintegration. The separation removes the individual from his former status; transition removes the barriers to the new status and reintegration marks the acceptance of his new status. In a wedding ceremony, separation is symbolized by the veil and isolation of the bride, transition by the noisy going-away rites and the honeymoon; and reintegration by the newly-married couple moving into their house, the bride being ritually lifted over the threshold into a new life.

Anthropologists and psychologists have used van Gennep's insights in their studies of primitive ritual, particularly of initiation rites, but their attitudes have often been at variance. Social anthropologists are concerned with the social aspects of the ceremonies, with their role as concrete symbols of status changes and community solidarity. A funeral ceremony, for example, establishes the precise status of the dead person as a spirit, and the status of his heirs and widows. It is a social rite, and while its ostensible object is the dead person, the primary beneficiaries are the living. Psychologists on the other hand are interested in understanding the consciousness of individuals, and therefore often discuss the Freudian themes of catharsis, castration anxiety, Oedipal conflicts, sexuality. An anthropologist explains circumcision as an arbitrary symbol of a boy's transition into adult manhood. A psychologist may claim that the mutilation of the penis symbolizes the final cutting of the umbilical cord, the child's final separation from the womb-mother; at puberty, boys must give up close attachment to their mothers, renounce childish feminine ways and desires and accept the adult male role. Or, a psychologist may suggest that the circumcision or the subincision of the penis is an attempt by men to make the penis resemble women's genitals because they envy their reproductive powers. In some Black Australian initiation rites, cases of ritual sodomy have been observed. An anthropologist explains these homosexual relations as a symbolic enactment of the rigid social hierarchy between old men (the active partners) and the younger adolescents (the passive partners). A psychologist says that this ritual sexuality reveals the intimate desires of individuals; or he may suggest that since the initiated youths are about to leave the world of women and children this sexual act shows that it is the last time the child will be treated as a woman.

I am first and foremost an anthropologist and I am wary of an approach that uses Black Australian symbolic behaviour to prove Freudian theories of the unconscious. Mistakenly, Freud likened ritual to his patients' obsessional symptoms that were a pathological counterpart to the formation of religion, and he described neurosis as a private religious system, and a religion as a universal obsessional neurosis. I believe that ritual and ceremony are basic to humanity, creating and sustaining social structures and maintaining an individual's sense of reality. Ritual may be, but often is not, an empty shell, merely a residue of beliefs whose functions are lost in the past; it should be an element essential to human survival. To try and show our basic need for ritual, I shall take a close look at Black and White symbolic behaviour, using an eclectic approach, at once anthropological and psychological. I shall try to understand both the sentiments of individuals and the patterns of community behaviour in an attempt to decipher universal patterns in Black and White – in 'primitive' and 'civilized' – behaviour during the ceremonies of passage rites. In this book, the Whites are the representatives of Euro-American culture who happen to live on the Australian continent and they generally practise christian baptism, monogamous marriage and believe in menopause and romantic love. The Blacks are the original inhabitants of the continent; they practise bloody initiation rites, polygynous marriage and believe in reincarnation and totemic spirits.

Today, White Australians are very curious about

themselves. By holding up a mirror to the seemingly exotic actions of the Blacks' way of life, we shall find not only insight, but a real delight in understanding the different ways people do the same thing and an excitement in sharing the life of a fascinating people. We may gain a new vision of ourselves as the exotic becomes credible and coherent and we look afresh at our long-accepted practices. Strange as it may appear at first sight, in describing initiation rites, the couvade, widow inheritance and infanticide, we shall begin to make sense of White Australian attitudes to the police, the Oedipus complex, old age and abortion.

This is a very personal book. Sometimes when I write 'White Australian' or 'westerner' the only appropriate point of reference may be myself; but I suppose this is an improvement on the usual anthropological theorizing about the 'Bumulu' or the 'primitive' which has no exact reference at all. And ironically, although author of a book which advocates a greater ceremonialization of the biological rhythms of life, I am an unfortunate example of a body and a life untouched by superstitious rite. I have never been christened or baptized, confirmed or married. I have no children. I have received no christian sacrament and my body is as unmutilated as that of an African divine king (apart from the absence of one canine tooth). The only ceremonial passages of any significance have been social ones – military, academic and ranking. The army ripped me from a cosy home and a doting mother and tried to make a man of me by cutting off my hair, putting me in a uniform and teaching me military rites. I passed exams at school and university. And to make up for my lamentable lack of status I was given a title in the ranking system of a mountain community in Cameroon, West Africa.

As an anthropologist my ostensible aim over the past years has been to make sense of behaviour patterns in exotic communities. While doing this, I also began to take a second and a third look at my own attitudes and assumptions. The innocent questions put to me by Africans forced me to climb out of my close-fitting cultural skin. Why wasn't I married? Why did I do woman's work? Why have I abandoned my widowed mother in Tasmania? What was my great-grand-father's name and where is his precious skull? Am I able to have normal sex without being circumcised?

Habits and patterns buried in the normal and every day behaviour of a westerner suddenly became unexplainable. Instead of being the big, white god, the wealthy anthropologist, the man in the trousers and with the magical books, I became an unfortunate child. I was a child to these Africans because although I seemed physically mature, I had never married and become a father. I was a woman because I dug the garden and cooked my own yams; and I was a woman because I had not had my foreskin, which represented a vagina, removed. In fact I was not even a human being as I had never been christened or given a name by my legitimate parents in any religious ceremony.

At first I did not care about my inhumanity, having all the brash self-confidence of the European living among the charming natives. I knew that it was usual for the people of one culture to consider the people of another as 'not quite human'. Nevertheless, after many years of struggling to understand various non-western cultures and undergoing the so-called and much over-rated culture shocks, I have now come to the rather unoriginal conclusion, that in comparative terms, the behaviour and attitudes of westerners in Tasmania, Ayrshire, Florida and Zürich are just as exotic as 'customs' of the Bumulu or the Black Australians of central Australia. Moreover, in ruthlessly objective terms, the day-to-day behaviour of modern Americans or Australians may be exposed as child-like, misguided and pagan – all the epithets once heaped on the scape-goat primitive's head.

When I was fifteen I made the puny discovery that there is no god, and I decided once and for all that everything associated with the supernatural was a fraud, particularly the empty rituals of christening, marriage and death. This realization was also partly due to fear as I had just attended my sister's adult baptism in the local church – the floor had opened up and the minister in thigh boots had ducked a trembling line of neophytes in four feet of water. Thirty years later, of course, I regret my 'discovery' and I regret my innocence of ritual and ceremony but there is no way of turning back. In studying other peoples I learned that life is not a hundred metre sprint from one field to the next but a delicately arranged progression from one status to the next, punctuated by meaningful rites. The Black Australian is a spirit, then a spirit-foetus, a named child, a weaned child, a circumcised youth, a married man, a father. Life is a cycle sanctioned by periodic ceremonies which culminate in the funeral of an old man who becomes a spirit again. White Australians may enjoy the thin sacraments of birth, marriage and death if they are christians and even if they are not; but on the whole we float nervously through life and into the black hole of death as non-returnable entities.

As an anthropologist teaching in western universities, I taught students that in simple face-to-face societies where people live in small groups and share few roles and statuses, it is easy to mark the physical and social stages of life by giving them ceremonial and public recognition. In Africa an unmarried woman, a married woman, a widow, a woman who has lost her child may wear special hairstyles to mark their status; a sexually mature youth is circumcised and a father of twins wears a particular necklace. I taught, and I believed, that the roles of a western adult were too complex to be displayed on their bodies; we have too many statuses to parade them in public all the time or mark them on our body or ceremonialize them. If my father is a policeman and a football referee and the judge at the local dahlia show, he has a different uniform for each of these different roles. My father did not wear a ring to show that he was married or have a special hairdo to show he had lost his only daughter. Black Australians too have different roles, and as these are performed before the same audience, conflict is avoided by marking these statuses and roles with ritual, bodily mutilation and special names. A Black Australian may have fifteen names marking fifteen different passage rites into fifteen statuses; we male westerners do not even change our names when we reach adolescence, get married and have our first male child. We are not allowed passage rites because our society is too complex!

Complexity in western industrialized society is the reason given for our refusal to acknowledge various critical moments, such as the period of adolescence. We are involved in so many shifting roles that no moment can be delineated as the magical point of entry into adulthood. According to the needs of society, usually decided by the state, young men and women are declared grown up at twelve or eighteen or twenty-one. Depending on the activity – riding a motorbike, smoking cigarettes, copulating, marrying, going to war, electing governments, being struck off father's tax rebate form – adulthood occurs at several different ages. Rituals of adolescence and maturity therefore would be pointless. However physical changes are not only not celebrated, they are positively ignored. Confirmation is one of the christian sacraments that today has the least meaning. It is a rite that is frequently administered when physical maturity occurs, but the fact of this simultaneity has never been stated, and therefore the social impact of confirmation is minimal and has value solely for the church. In other societies adolescent ritual has meaning in terms of attitudes to adulthood and sexuality; even the bar mitzvah is a ritual acknowledgement of the adult male jew.

Anthropologists, victims of a primitive thought process that demands binary oppositions, have long accepted a division between primitive and civilized, sometimes changing the words to small-scale and large-scale, industrial and pre-industrial. In terms of technology and the harnessing of energy these words may have some meaning. In terms of personal life, particularly the adjustment to changes in an individual's life cycle, his sexuality and maturation, they can have none. It cannot be true that we are doomed to go through the periods of adolescence, menopause, dying in unbearable privacy simply because we live in 'civilized', 'large-scale', 'industrial' society. It is sometimes assumed that modern western civilization does not need ritual because there are few occasions for fear and distress as civil order guarantees us freedom from the danger of abuse, disease and famine. Primitive society needs ritual because life is a round of fearful encounters and risks that must be magically counteracted or warded off. The smug idea here is that we are the rational masters of a controlled environment and that individuals and groups are therefore not afflicted by moments of uncertainty and doubt, as are 'primitives' who are buffeted by the storms of technological incompetence. The environments of the desert hunter and the urban worker in the west may appear very different at first sight, but uncertainty is a plague in both of them. In the desert, fear for survival is constant, and magic is used to help Black Australians through drought and famine as well as through life's passages. The urban worker is not dependent on rain or other climatic factors, but he fears for his survival and is the victim of such uncontrollable things as price fluctuations, the European Economic Community's buying programme, a strike in Japan.

I maintain that everyone needs supernatural beliefs. Most contemporary western prophets see the deritualization of life – but not ceremonies of state – as inevitable. Many of them, following Freud, consider all aspects of religion a kind of community neurosis. Ritual is an empty waste of time and money, a perfunctory habit left over from the bad old days. Sex and good health are all we need. While I agree that the symbols of christianity may have lost their meaning for most of us, I do not think we should necessarily forego the ceremonies and rites of status changes. In this book I comment on the near universality of these passage rites, a universality which is derived from the basic biological nature of the changes involved. And this universality is paralleled by a similarity in the patterns of symbolic behaviour: the idea of withdrawal, transition and return in many of the rites, the significance of the colours red, black and white, the repetition of universal elements such as lustration, the recurrence of bodily mutilation, the special clothes, the public acclamation, the symbolic food, the bells and the drums. I believe that if most of the world's cultures celebrate passages by rituals, feasts and patterned symbolic behaviour, we must try to find out why and think twice before advising our children, our friends and our students to give them up. It is meaningless to say that western life is 'complex' or that rituals are 'empty'.

Part One
Passage to Life

Chapter One
Becoming a Mother

The first of life's passages – birth – usually involves three main actors: the mother, the father and the child, and Black and White Australians have their very special ways of celebrating the physical and social aspects of coming into being. Throughout the world the passage of birth is surrounded by a luxuriance of special medical and magical precautions; the latter preponderate in all societies except our own because generally the issue of a successful birth is in doubt and the hazards involved are tremendous.

In fact the most dangerous and traumatic of all life's crises is the first one ever made – the physical passage of the child from the womb to the outside world. Childbirth is dangerous and very painful in human beings primarily because of the evolutionary specialization of our bodies due to our curious upright posture. The female physique is constitutionally ill-adapted to easy, carefree childbirth. The excessive growth of the size of the brain makes the baby's head big and awkward and birth is not only a painful experience for the mother, but also for the child. Some psychologists have gone so far as to argue that the experience leaves deep mental scars that explain most adult psychotic behaviour. Because of the violent ejection of the over-sized head through the narrow birth canal, many people have a permanent nostalgia for the relatively roomy womb and a desire to return there. This nostalgia, which remains with us till death, is reflected in our panicky horror of the dark tunnels, passages and caves.

Because of the physical difficulty of birth there can be no such thing as totally 'natural' childbirth. Not only parturition but procreation and pregnancy are bound to arouse such strong emotions in all peoples that 'having a baby' is never a straightforward business simply of copulation, fertilization, the growth of the foetus and its expulsion. Natural behaviour is everywhere embellished by magical behaviour – special taboos, rituals, even body painting and mutilations – that emphasizes the dangerous state of the pregnant woman and the new-born child and in some cases the father as well. Taboos are thought to protect the mother and the child and their close associates from supernatural harm; food prescriptions and special diets for the expectant mother are designed to ease childbirth or to mark the special nature of the mother and her child.

The pregnant woman, and then the new mother (the puerpera), is a delicate creature in a delicate physical and supernatural state; in many societies she is not only considered vulnerable to dangerous magical forces but also harmful to other people. In modern Greece, where many traditional practices are still observed, the new mother, known as the *lechona*, is both in danger and dangerous. Her confinement is hedged about with taboos designed to secure her and others from harm. In Ancient Greece, the mother was considered polluted through childbirth and the baby had to be washed to purify him. The lechona in classical Greece was excluded from the temple for forty days and visitors to her childbed were thought to be polluted by her.

Oddly enough the actual moment of birth, the most perilous moment for mother and child, is rarely ritualized as a crisis passage in itself – possibly because of the high mortality rate of new-born babies in all societies except the twentieth-century west. One of the rare rituals which affects the baby as soon as it is born is our custom of the midwife's slap, a gesture of 'welcome' which in some parts of the United States is repeated at every birthday: at birth one slap, at one year two slaps, at ten years eleven slaps. However this uniquely violent gesture is confined to us and is indeed a strange way of welcoming the baby which has just successfully traversed the traumatic womb to world passage.

A few days or weeks after the birth the real rituals begin to convert the foetus-child into a human child and the husband and wife into the mother and father. Only when the immediate danger of mortality is passed does the child receive its 'baptism' into the world of human beings; then it is circumcised or named or christened, or otherwise marked as a cultural rather than a natural member of society. The mother may receive a special name or arrange her hair in a particular way. The father is congratulated by kith and kin and may change his own name, often through the custom of teknonymy – being called 'father of so-and-so' in recognition of his new status. Throughout the post-natal period there are usually ritual restrictions on sex between the mother and father of the child; these range from complete abstinence for several years to the mildest of injunctions during the first weeks of lactation as is the case in White Australia and other western societies.

Attitudes to pregnancy

Black Australians lay great stress on fertility and reproduction in both animals and humans and most of their sacred ritual is concerned with increase. Unlike their White sisters, all Black women are expected to have as many children as possible and as soon as possible. Since motherhood is their major, their most valued, their most satisfying role, all girls are married young, often before puberty and have their first babies at fourteen, fifteen or sixteen. Childless women are considered unfortunate and after a number of unproductive years are called by the same name as women who have reached the menopause. Since Black Australian women achieve status as mothers or not at all, the women themselves dread sterility and explain it as a punishment meted out from a supernatural spirit. A woman without children is a 'lazy woman' who has made no effort to induce a spirit-child to enter her womb. Sterility may be explained as the result of incorrect behaviour: perhaps as a young girl she playfully tied on a man's hair waistband. This tabooed action is thought to cause cramps in the internal organs, making the womb incapable of expanding sufficiently to receive a spirit-child.

Once pregnant the Black woman takes a multitude of symbolic precautions to avoid ritual dangers. She is vulnerable to attack from the rainbow spirit and for this reason she is not allowed to bathe in large ponds or to gaze on large stretches of water; should she go out in rainy weather, she must protect herself and her baby by painting her body with yellow ochre. Black women also observe rigid food taboos; a pregnant girl is warned by older relatives not to eat the meat of dangerous, spiky animals or strong-tasting vegetables. Having eaten tabooed food can be the reason for a difficult birth or a less-than-perfect baby. Rejection of meat is common because the mother does not want the baby to be marked like an animal or to take on beast-like characteristics. Nor does she want the foetus to grow huge on a heavy protein diet and thus create problems at delivery. The husband may share these ritual precautions: together the future parents refuse bitter yams, the spiny echidna, the large-clawed possum, the spike-tailed lizard. Certain groups have special taboos: an Aranda husband may not use his boomerang during his wife's pregnancy or kill large and dangerous game with his spear.

The Black expectant mother is in a delicate supernatural condition; the White woman sees herself in a delicate physical condition. Yet her attitudes and demands are just as illogical and irrational as Black Australian food taboos. A White woman might refuse hot curries, strongly flavoured meat, lumpy custards or eggs. She may give up smoking and alcohol and the smell of coffee may make her sick. These are not, unfortunately, precise ritual taboos but they do help define the special social – not physical – status of the mother to be. Cravings may reflect certain deficiencies in the diet, but this scientific explanation is insufficient. Throughout the world special behaviour, frequently to do with food, is the expression of society's need to emphasize the special nature of pregnancy and the special situation of the pregnant woman. Black Australians have rigid ritual behaviour; White Australians call attention to their state by special clothes or capricious demands for unusual, expensive or difficult-to-get food. The pregnant White woman, lacking precise taboos, becomes 'ill' and must receive solicitous behaviour from husband and kin.

Pregnant Black women avoid the spiny anteater, the rainbow spirit and special spirit places; pregnant White women often specifically avoid horror films, deformed neighbours and street accidents. My mother went to the extreme of looking at beautiful pictures, calm landscapes of whispering gums, and beautiful babies in order to produce the beautiful, calm baby girl of her dreams. Other women go to concerts or read uplifting literature as the extra-physical experience is thought to influence the child in the womb. And they avoid disturbing incidents: a few hundred years ago a woman in Guilford, England, was said to have brought forth a litter of rabbits after being frightened by one. Recent studies in America have shown that not only the physical but also the psychological state of the mother-to-be can affect the foetus – too much stress can cause malformation or defects in the nervous system of the infant. Keeping cheerful and calm in pleasant conditions – attending art galleries and eating special food, avoiding the big-clawed possum and the rainbow snake – may be good advice for both Black and White pregnant women.

Birth of the child

Among Black Australians, the physical facts of pregnancy and the birth of the child itself are treated naturally enough, without fuss or special medical attention. The woman is in no sense an invalid and continues her daily routine of collecting small game and plant food until delivery is imminent. Pregnant women show no concern when the child is expected: it will come in 'god's good time' and labour pains often catch them unawares while on a food-gathering expedition a long way from camp.

Birth always takes place outside the main camp. There are no specialist midwives as such, but most older women are fully experienced. Female relatives massage the woman's belly to find out which way the baby is lying, and they make sure the head comes foremost. I found very few details in the literature on the facts of birth, probably because birth is very much a private affair of the women and kept secret from their own menfolk and from inquisitive White observers who, in the early years, were always men.

Most observers claim that delivery for a Black woman is

a straightforward business. Despite their slim, narrow frames, the baby arrives quickly and usually without complications. Relaxed and quick deliveries are probably due to psychological incentive – they know they must give birth without medical help – and to their good muscular development. However, having heard of the difficulties among African women and of frequent deaths during labour in primitive conditions, I am wary of blithe remarks about primitive women experiencing easy childbirth. African women in turn are convinced that European women have access to secret and magical methods of easy childbirth.

The Black woman gives birth in the most natural position: kneeling or squatting. To alleviate pain, hot leaves are applied to her back and groin or an older woman presses her thumbs against the eyes of the woman in labour. When it is born, the baby is cleaned in a special dust or fungus powder mixed with urine. An older woman holds the baby and moulds the head into shape; she may also heat her fingers in the fire and push back a boy-child's penis with her thumb 'so that it should not hang too low'; sometimes she puts a centipede on the penis 'otherwise it will jump up every time it sees a woman'. The old woman may also massage the baby-girl's clitoris with warm fingers, pressing it down so that it should never become embarrassingly big.

The umbilical cord is cut with a digging stick or stone knife: apparently the bleeding ceases quickly and the risk of infection is lessened by the strong ultra-violet rays of the sun. The placenta is expelled by foot pressure on the uterus. The umbilical cord is sometimes tied around the child's neck and the placenta put in a hole and covered up, and a fire lit over it. Among the Aranda, the cord is cut off by the mother who wraps it in fur string and makes it into a necklace for the child: this is its first clothing. The necklace is supposed to facilitate the growth of the child, keeping it quiet and averting illness in general and helping 'to deaden the child's ears to the noise of barking of the camp dogs'.

When the fire lit over the placenta has died down, the mother squats over it to let the smoke dry up the lochia, a bloody menstrual-like fluid. Afterwards she rests with the child and neither of them takes any food. On the second day she suckles the child and her women attendants let out great celebratory shouts of joy. Five days after the birth, the women return to the camp in triumph and present the baby to its father and to the rest of the community.

It is uncommon throughout the world for babies to be born in the home. Black Australians send the woman to the bush. White Australians send her to hospital to have her baby with the sick and dying. A pregnant woman in White Australia is a sick woman; the Black woman does not consider pregnancy an illness or even noticeably debilitating; in contrast to the great attention paid to her supernatural health, there is a general nonchalance about her physical condition. The White woman is very conscious of her physical condition: she visits her doctor regularly and often rests for long periods. She gives up strenuous exercise and often does not play sport: the Victorian and New South Wales women's squash associations, for example, will not allow a pregnant woman to play pennant squash. In this way White Australian culture uses 'illness' instead of magic to call attention to a pregnant woman's condition. The first symptom of pregnancy is often morning 'sickness', a nausea which probably has more symbolic and psychological value than physiological necessity; even White fathers-to-be may experience morning sickness though rarely does either parent acknowledge the irrational symbolism of such 'illness'. Interestingly enough, 'morning sickness' occurs much more frequently with first pregnancies than with later ones: the first time a couple becomes mother and a father obviously has far greater significance than subsequent times.

In many ways, a hospital is a much stranger place to have a baby than the bush. The healthy pregnant woman is exposed to infection in a place devoted to curing diseases; once the fatalities due to infection were greater than childbirth complications. Nurses go from diseased patients to healthy women having babies, and from women recuperating from childbirth to others who have just begun labour pains. After delivery the highly infectious lochia is discharged. The Black woman discharges the lochia in the smoke of a fire in isolation; in a modern hospital White women discharging lochia after the birth of the child are housed in the same quarters as those who are about to give birth.

Hospitals have become terrifyingly antiseptic places. Parturition takes place in cold hygienic secrecy away from close female relatives, in the presence of starched nurses, a male doctor, a frightened husband and perhaps some giggling students. Black Australians, delivering their babies in the bush, follow a more common pattern of childbirth; White Australians, North Americans and Europeans have developed a barbarous and inhuman method of bringing their women to childbed.

The White mother has her baby in a reclining position, not to facilitate delivery but to facilitate the work of the doctor. Births are more and more often artificially induced, and painkillers, antiseptics and anaesthetics remove the mother more and more from the sensations of birth; the number of Caesarean births is increasing at a rate that medical evidence can hardly justify. Episiotomies are almost always performed; episiotomy is the medical term for the western practice of making an incision in the perineum as the baby descends the birth canal. An odd ritual, practised also by Hottentots in Africa, it is a primitive bodily mutilation which can result in appreciable blood loss and discomfort from surgical stitches. There can also be a considerable amount of pain on the resumption of intercourse since this birth mutilation takes time to heal and sometimes severs muscles and erectile tissues involved in the delicate response of sex. Despite these problems, White Australian women accept and even demand the operation, believing a tear will result unless the clean cut is made. In fact, an episiotomy is usually unnecessary, as unnecessary clinically as the painful stretching of a Black Australian girl's vagina prior to first intercourse with her husband. Both operations serve as physical markings of an important occasion (in one case birth and in the other, first intercourse after marriage) that is part of a pattern of symbolic behaviour surrounding the critical passage rites of sex and birth.

Birth is an important passage rite for parents and child, and since passage rites are often marked by physical mutilation it might not be too far-fetched to suggest that the cutting of the vaginal tissue and even Caesarean births have as important a symbolic value as circumcision, scarification, clitoridectomy. 'Hygiene theorists' may scoff, and declare that it is in the interests of women and progress that surgery be performed at this time. Induction, injections, episiotomy and Caesarean sections are modern methods of efficient childbirth. I made some enquiries and was told that, on the whole, induction and surgical births are carried out for the convenience of the doctor and the woman.

I suggest that Caesarean births, induction and episiotomy must be viewed not only on their medical merits but also as part of a new western social philosophy requiring an unnatural acceleration of labour in childbirth; none of these techniques, of course, were known to Black women. We may reasonably doubt whether these mutilations at birth are biologically necessary to a woman who is encouraged to take birth naturally, relaxing and pushing and allowing her vagina to stretch in the slow but normal mammalian manner. To suggest that episiotomy is nothing more than a primitive body mutilation, a physical mark symbolizing motherhood may seem wildly exaggerated to some people. Yet when they read of similar surgery among Hottentots or Black- Australians, they accept its illogical and symbolic nature. When I was young, it was the fashion to circumcise male babies who were a few days old; this fashion was fiercely justified by the hygiene theorists. The fashion has passed; circumcision was an ideal method for mothers to mark the fact of matrescence on their male children, a physical sign of her status as 'mother of a male child'. Now, hospitals do not offer foreskin removal as a fashionable mutilation: they offer an operation on the mother's body in the form of a vaginal cut.

The point is that birth is never natural; human societies develop complex birth procedures to accentuate the social and psychological importance of the event. Certain types of food are considered improper for parturient and lactating women. A nursing woman in hospital for example is usually given symbolic food, food for an invalid. Before the birth she is advised not to drink or eat too much; if she must eat she is offered thin bread and butter with jellied jam, strained chicken broth and sieved meat and fish, light food without hard lumps or gristle. In many ways the mother is given the kind of food the baby itself might manage, hardly a rational approach to childbirth when labour is often hard and long – often the hardest work some western women ever do. The hygiene theory for starving a woman before birth is that if something goes wrong and a general anaesthetic has to be administered, vomiting may occur and the woman may inhale her own vomitus. My personal theory is that special foods, like the Black Australian food taboos, and 'unnatural' operations, like Black Australian body mutilations, have important symbolic value at the time of important passage rites such as matrescence.

A White Australian woman has her baby while being attended by specialists; her mother, grandmother, aunts and sisters play no role as they do in Black Australia. On the other hand, there has recently been a unique development in western countries: the husband is encouraged to attend the birth of his children. Although the Black father takes a great interest in the proceedings and follows a precise ritual, he is always forbidden to approach the scene of birth. Once again the Black Australian mode is the usual one, the White almost unique in ethnography. Formerly the White Australian father also stayed at home; today he is given an unprecedented role and may be the first human being the baby claps eyes on. What are the reasons behind the husband's presence during childbirth and his playing a role traditionally reserved to grandmothers, aunts and female cousins?

At first glance it appears that the White husband is undergoing a kind of couvade (see page 53): being present at the delivery of his child emphasizes his paternal role. However, the husband is not becoming a father but rather a second or surrogate mother. He accompanies the new mother home from the hospital and it is he – rather than a female servant, a nanny or a female relative – who helps feed baby, wash baby, nurse baby, change baby. In our world of isolated families, the husband is being forced into a maternal or at least an 'aunty' role. Many men now have more free time at home and their wives have jobs, with the result that fathers become mothers. Present at the birth, the father's female role begins at once. In some Australian hospitals, if the mother is out of action for a long period after a Caesarean birth, the baby is encouraged to learn to suckle on the milkless nipples of its father–mother; in Black Australia these nipples would be those of a female relative. The new western family has a female and a male mother; both parents wield the napkin and the bottle and the child is sometimes confused and calls both parents 'Mummy'.

A Black Australian father is very definitely a father, not a mother, but he expresses his interest in the birth of his child from a safe distance. While his wife is in labour, the Aranda husband remains in the men's camp where he takes off his hair girdle, often his only clothing, and gives it to a woman who takes it to the spot where the women are gathered for the birth. It is tied tightly around his wife's body just under her breasts. The husband does not speak until the child is delivered; if it is delayed he will walk very slowly up and down opposite the place where the women are waiting, with a view to persuade the unborn child to follow him. This behaviour is very similar to the traditional behaviour in western countries where the husband waits nervously at home untying knots and opening the door or pacing up and down the hospital corridor. Among another central Australian people, the Walbiri, the father-to-be also strips naked and rubs his thumb down the side of his nose or under his arm, and draws a red-ochre stripe from his chest to his navel; this action, by sympathetic magic, is thought to facilitate the birth. If the baby does not arrive he is told by the women to sit alone and think hard of his wife's pain and trouble; when the child is born he puts on his armbands and headband and returns to the camp.

Mother and child

The Black mother and her baby return to the camp after a few days of seclusion. They are presented to a joyous community: the baby is painted with charcoal and the mother with a red stripe down the centre of her body, front and back, while the lower half of her face, from the bridge of her nose downwards, is painted black. This ceremony celebrates the passage rite of parenthood. The new family, mother and father and child, sleep in a special place in the camp; a fire between the father and mother symbolizes the sexual taboo for the next few months or years between a man and his nursing mother-wife. The baby sleeps close to its mother, cradled in the curve of her body. Both mother and child are cosseted by all the women of the community and the baby is cuddled and breast-fed by all its 'mothers' who clean it thoroughly in the first few weeks with a mixture of dust and milk. The baby is encouraged to grow by a gentle massaging and pulling of the arms and legs.

The White Australian mother also undergoes a passage rite of the same kind, a ceremonial progression from labour pains and birth (separation), a period of recuperation in hospital (transition) and then reintegration into the community. While she is pregnant and giving birth she is set aside from normal mortals, given special foods and her body mutilated. After a transitional period in hospital she returns as a mother with a host of celebratory cards and congratulations from relatives and friends. In some religious communities she may be 'churched': the woman who has given birth may be considered polluting for a certain period, and a ritual removes this 'filth' a few days or weeks after delivery. Traditionally a jewish woman was unclean for a week after the birth of a girl and for two weeks after the birth of a boy. Modern White Australian mothers have no concept of ritual impurity, yet matrescence is always celebrated in some way. A visitor to small-town Australia will be surprised at the space in the local newspaper devoted to photographs of new mothers and their children, pages of tired ladies in maternity nighties sitting awkwardly on hospital beds holding newborn, barely recognizable babies.

As in all passage rites, mothers, Black and White, are in an in-between, transitional state for a period. The White woman stays in hospital and then goes home with her husband to assume full responsibility for her child; the Black woman stays in the bush for five days. The baby also goes through a transitional period of a few days or a few weeks before it becomes integrated into the community, before it (not yet 'he' or 'she') becomes fully human. In many societies, particularly where infant mortality is high, the baby remains unnamed during this transition period; if this neutral, non-human child dies it is buried without ceremony. Black Australians maintain that becoming human is a gradual process; the child's soul is thought to enter the foetus while it is still in the womb, leaving the totemic centre of the father's clan and entering his wife through the vagina or a crack in her foot. As far as the Black Australians are concerned the foetus is spiritual rather than material; it only becomes material after birth. Women who have miscarriages are therefore unconvinced that the foetus was human, but think that it must have been an animal that entered her womb by mistake. The Black child becomes fully human when the father gives it a name: not his own name or the name of his clan, but a unique personal name.

The formal 'naming' or christening of a child is also the ritual moment when the White child becomes part of the human group. Traditionally baptism is accompanied by a feast and the parents are publicly acknowledged as 'father' and 'mother'. Christian baptism once involved the full array of godparents, priest, friends, relatives, special clothes, presents and parties. Now, the baby's naming is often celebrated merely by an announcement in the paper or few congratulatory cards. However there is always a rite of some kind, since it is a universal fact that parturition as such is never enough to turn a baby into a human being or a man and woman into 'father' and 'mother'.

Two other types of ritual accompany childbirth: one marks the father as legitimate progenitor of the child; the other safeguards the health and spirit of the child. In Black Australia both are achieved in one rite when the father formally gives the child its name, which becomes a sacred possession and is not easily revealed and is rarely used. Black Australians take on a dozen, even twenty names during their lifetime;

each one marks an important event in his life, but the first name, the personal name is never used in the presence of its owner and never uttered in the company of others 'because of shame'. White Australians on the other hand are bold with people's names and are expected to hand over their personal christian name to the most casual acquaintance. 'Hello!' says the lady in the hotel. 'I'm Lil, what's your name?' A moment's nervous hesitation. 'Robert.' 'Glad to meet you Bert.' Quite different from a Black Australian who finds it as difficult to tell his private, sacred baptismal name as a White Australian does to obey a request to remove all his clothes in the town's main street for a summary medical inspection.

How do people who have given up formal baptisms celebrate patrescence and matrescence, and mark the ensoulment of the child – endowment of the physical body with the status of 'human member of the community'? In Australia I went to one informal celebration of this moment of reintegration. The mother and father, an uneccentric, straightforward middle-class couple, were unwilling to have their first child baptized according to church ritual so they invited their friends and a few relatives of the same age to a party at their home. Although this celebration lacked precise ritual formula, symbolic behaviour served to express the change of status of husband and wife into father and mother, and the child was presented to a gathering of the community. Inside the house the mother and her friends sat among dozens of congratulatory cards from neighbours and kin; she had prepared a table laden with cakes and puddings; for much of the evening she suckled and showed off her baby. The father stood outside on the terrace between the sacred barrel and the sacred barbecue offering beer and sausages to his friends. The symbolic behaviour involved – the public exhibition of paternal virility and maternal fertility with appropriate foods – is obvious and attractive. Towards the end of the evening after the women had come outside and eaten male virility food, the men joined the women inside and ate some female fertility food. The party went on inside the house, and the father awkwardly nursed his first baby to the merriment of his mates.

The naming or baptism of a child in Black Australia has another important meaning. Before this time if the baby dies, it does not receive a formal funeral; it may also be killed without moral reprobation. Infanticide was almost the only means Black Australians had of controlling population. Abortion was possibly attempted but technical knowledge assuring results was not available. Traditional forms of contraception were limited to a few herbs and special songs which young girls used to sing if they were unwilling to become pregnant too soon; like White Australian girls they like a little fun before settling down. While Westerners are capable of inducing miscarriages, have invented condoms and the Pill, Black Australians have had to face the painful necessity of killing a child if there was not enough food, if it was born while another child was still in need of the breast, or if it was born deformed or mentally deficient. In all cases of infanticide the child is killed immediately after its birth – before it has 'become human' and before the mother feels any affection for it. Infanticide is never undertaken lightly and as a rule both parents have to sanction the killing, which is usually done by an older woman who hits the new-born with a stone or suffocates it in the sand. Fortunately the women can comfort themselves with the knowledge that the child's spirit returns to the particular totemic field from whence it came and will be born again.

Babies are killed out of necessity, not maternal whim, and after the first day the baby is never killed. These simple facts should be kept in mind because travellers, missionaries and charitable ladies have spread lurid stories of Black women going through pregnancy and labour in order to kill their children and share them with their friends in the bush. This was one explanation given by missionaries to account for the sad fact that in some tribes – already demoralized by the presence of christian Whites – years had passed without the survival of a single child. Yet in the same breath these rumour-mongers recounted stories of pathetic Black mothers who carried their dead babies around with them in bark bundles for months before the relatives could persuade them to give up the beloved corpse and bury it.

To an impartial observer it will be clear that Black infanticide parallels White contraception and abortion, and exists in order to control population in the face of environmental pressures without denying personal sexual desires. Westerners have used a variety of techniques – celibacy, various non-productive sexual perversions, legalized abortion and the Pill – to achieve the same goals. Our view of 'callous and inhuman' depends on how we see our own actions and those of other peoples with less technical know-how. White Australians accept the hanging of murderers and are willing to send their children to die in other people's wars. Before more advanced techniques of birth control were publicized, there were innumerable cases in Tasmania in the 1930s and 1940s of ignorant young girls being charged before the court as criminals because they had abandoned new-born babies in lavatories, dustbins or rubbish heaps. In western society, a large percentage of the population considers abortion and contraception a crime and a sin; fortunately the moral and practical necessity of infanticide in Black Australia is considered painful but is not imbued with feelings of guilt.

In both Black and White Australia there is a close connection between infanticide (or abortion) and the declared moment when the born or unborn child becomes fully 'human'. Since Black Australians have no efficient techniques of contraception or abortion, they allow a limbo period when unwanted children may be killed without moral guilt. In the west, the problem has become more difficult because of more efficient methods of abortion, and our moral tutors – the church, state and newspapers – are trying to come to terms with it by defining the moment when the foetus becomes human. By the late nineteenth century, the Roman Catholic church took the view that ensoulment began at conception although the early church had maintained that it did not begin until the quickening or about the sixteenth week. Today Catholic doctors and nurses are forbidden to make a direct attack on the foetus even to save the mother, and manuals tell doctors how to decide difficult cases and priests what to do with the foetus after a stillbirth. A stillborn child is conditionally baptized, and if a foetus is not expected to survive it is baptized 'intra-uterine'. The other extreme, promoted by the women's liberation movement, is that the foetus has no independent status of its own and its destiny may be decided by the mother. The state usually takes a position midway, allowing abortion during the first twenty-four weeks of pregnancy.

The Black Australian position is certainly less specious, less casuistic than our own which is full of contradictions. As well as allowing the mother control over the foetus, courts in western society sometimes recognize the rights of the foetus itself: a woman may be sued in an English court if her child can prove it was injured in a car accident or by drugs due to negligence on the part of the mother; yet the mother may abort with impunity. Feminists maintain that the foetus is part of a woman's body. A Roman Catholic scientist may maintain that the ovaries lie in the wall of the ring the genital tract forms; when the ova are shed they are 'laid', as in all mammals, technically outside the body. The foetus is thus considered completely distinct from its mother from the moment of conception. Black Australians are unconcerned with religious polemic but they use a ritual occasion, five days after the baby's birth, to confirm its passage from eliminable neutral object to named, human child.

Chapter Two
Becoming a Father

Matrescence, or becoming a mother, is a much easier business than patrescence, or becoming a father. A woman's husband, who is usually but not always both pater and genitor of her children, often feels the need to stress by various means his social fatherly role (as pater) and his physical fatherly role (as genitor). White Australians tend to stress the physiological aspects of fatherhood as paternity suits show. Black Australians tend to find physical paternity uninteresting; for them it is important to become a father socially and spiritually.

Throughout Black Australia ideas about conception are imbued with the dogma that women are spiritually rather than physically fertilized through contact with a spirit-animal, a breeze, a particular stretch of water. Some people believe that spirit-children are placed in pools by the rainbow serpent; others that babies are incarnated in birds and fish and reptiles; still others believe that the spirits are in little frog-like animals that wander the countryside. Black Australians believe that conception occurs when one of these spirit-children enters the woman. And at the moment of conception, a churinga – a sacred stone or wood object associated with totems – is dropped to earth. When the child is born, the mother tells her husband, the child's father, the position of the tree or rock near when she supposes the spirit-child entered her. The father finds the churinga and keeps it for the child in a secret, sacred place. Associated with these ideas is that the Black Australian baby has been dreamed by its father – the man married to its mother – before it is conceived by a spirit associated with his clan and born to the woman.

To Black Australians, these beliefs in spiritual rather than physical paternity add an extra dimension to their 'humanness'; only animals and perhaps the more rational White

Australians, who believe that human beings are more natural than cultural, can be formed simply by the vulgar action of sexual intercourse. These facts must be borne in mind when people make disparaging remarks about Black Australians' ignorance of physical paternity. Spiritual and social paternity is of more significance to the Black father and child than the base fact of physical paternity.

Virgin birth

Similar ideas, of course, are found in traditional christianity. According to one case of Black Australian religious dogma, the spirit-child can enter the woman through a crack in her foot; in White Australian religious dogma it entered the Virgin Mary through her ear. Both Blacks and Whites, therefore, believe in a kind of 'virgin birth'. For Black Australians it is a matter of everyday occurrence. For many Whites it happened nearly 2000 years ago when Jesus Christ was magically conceived. What we have here are two examples of religious dogma relating not to matters of fact and reproduction, but to metaphysics and legitimacy. The 'virgin birth' of every Black Australian is a magical experience in the same way as the immaculate conception of Jesus Christ was a magical experience.

Anthropologists have long debated whether Black Australians are serious when they hotly deny any knowledge of the facts of physical paternity. Early observers and the first ethnographers were told categorically that sexual intercourse had nothing to do with conception. Sexual intercourse caused conception only among the lower animals. Higher animals – human beings and the kangaroo – became pregnant without the help of the sperm of a male partner. A Black Australian woman became pregnant because a spirit-child found its way into her womb.

And kangaroos? Among the weird and varied fauna of the Australian continent the Black Australian gives the marsupial kangaroo pride of place as totemic species, source of food, and social animal. At one with the environment, Black Australians observe the kangaroo and use their observations in their definition of what is human. The Australian continent is south-east of the so-called Wallace Line which means that placental mammals are rare; man, the dingo and a species of rat were unique in the marsupial world until Whites introduced others. The foetus is kept in the pouch of kangaroos and other Australian marsupials because of inferior development of the placenta. Despite its odd marsupial characteristics*, the kangaroo is man-like in that it has an upright posture, uses its forepaws like hands and has other human-like movements; Black Australians use it as a model for human behaviour rather like we use dogs.

The behaviour of the kangaroo confirms the Black Australian belief in parthenogenesis. The female kangaroo, as Black Australians noted, seems subject to post-partum conception: to all outward appearances, semen is unnecessary for conception and birth. Black hunters have broken the legs of wounded kangaroos and have captured and kept them in pasture; they observed that the female was capable of serial births without a male kangaroo mounting her. It seemed that a female kangaroo produced offspring according to the amount of pasture available. However, notwithstanding White Australian folklore that baby kangaroos in the pouch bud off their mother's teats, the female kangaroo does require impregnation by the male. Though the female is not able to carry and nurse more than two or three joeys at a time, the ovaries may release more eggs, all of which are fertilized at a single mating. The surplus fertilized eggs are held 'in reserve' and dropped in succession when there is plentiful pasture; the eggs develop and the babies are born as the older joeys become sufficiently mature to leave the pouch and fend for themselves. The Black Australian naturalist sees several parturitions over a long period – several

---

*Among these odd characteristics I include the pouch and the number and position of the orifices which make up the external sexual and excretory organs: the female has only one external orifice for excretion, copulation and birth; the male has testicles, a bifurcate penis with testicles above the penis and an anus. In both sexes the outlet of the bladder and the intestines connect and discharge into the cloaca.

virgin births – while the kangaroo is in captivity without access to males.

Had Black Australians observed certain polyps and crustacea, they would have noted genuine cases of virgin birth as both the octopus and the crab are capable of producing off-spring without fertilization; they do this in order to produce as many young as possible when there is a temporary excess of food supplies. Reproduction for these animals becomes sexual only when living conditions deteriorate. From animal behaviour scientists have learned that reproduction and sex as such serve very different functions: 'virginal' reproduction enables the extension and survival of the species while sexual reproduction allows the number of variations within the species to increase and provides a basis for the development of new types and eventually new species.

From animal behaviour Black Australians found their cherished beliefs confirmed. But, you will say, they are mistaken observations and mistaken beliefs of a deluded childlike people. This is prejudice. When a Black Australian happily talks of his totemic beliefs and declares that he is a kangaroo, we smile and pat his deluded head. When someone reads us the story about Helen of Troy whose father was a swan we hail it as a beautiful, civilized myth. When a Black Australian makes a statement about kangaroos or about virgin birth, he is talking about a myth, stating a theological belief of the same kind as the White Australian's conviction that the mother of Jesus Christ was a virgin. We accept our own myths as normal – these myths often tell of the same kind of magical conception of gods and heroes as those told by Black Australians to astonished Whites.

Black Australians love kangaroos; we love dogs and horses and choose these odd animals as models for our kind of 'human behaviour'. It is still believed in the racing world that a thoroughbred mare is spoilt forever for breeding purposes if she is first mounted by an ill-bred stallion; her subsequent foals will be tainted by this first unworthy substance. Dog-breeders think that a pure-bred bitch may be tainted if she is covered by a mongrel. Some kennel clubs have been known to refuse to register litters of a pure-bred bitch mated with a pure-bred dog if she once had a mongrel litter. From these cases, it seems that people concerned with scientific breeding have projected on to bitches and mares a variation of the basic, magical premise of christian sexuality and christian families: one-flesh, unadulterated monogamous marriage.

Westerners see animals as humans; Black Australians see humans as animals. Westerners have a magical belief in a kind of physical pollution whereby a woman's former lover may effect her offspring with the legal husband – like the mongrel dog and the pure-bred bitch. If a good christian marries and learns that his wife once lived with a yellow, red or black mongrel he may be convinced that his own pure sperm may be adulterated – the very word is significant – by his wife's former lover. The primitive belief here is that through a peculiar poly-paternal process, substances absorbed by the female genital tract (human, canine or equine) exert an influence on the embryos of subsequent matings. Aristotle too (expressed in his *History of Animals*) held such an idea: 'A certain woman, having committed adultery, brought forth one child resembling her husband and the other resembling her adulterous lover.' Similar magical beliefs in the nature of sperm and its contagious or polluting nature are revealed in the ancient English law that held that a man who seduced the wet nurse of the heir to the throne should be found guilty of contaminating the blood royal; it was believed that the liquid of ejaculation had some kind of magnetic connection with breast milk and it could therefore spoil the child. This kind of belief may explain White Australian women's reluctance to suckle other women's babies; Black women, less primitive here, hand their babies from breast to comforting breast without any irrational fears.

These examples may prevent us from cherishing fond ideas about our 'scientific' attitudes to reproduction, sex and childbirth. According to marriage counsellors, many White people are just as ignorant regarding sex and reproduction as Black Australians are purported to be. My mother, married in her teens, was convinced that her gold wedding ring had some magical role to play in conception. In an equally irrational way, some Black women have told anthropologists that they cannot conceive just by copulating; without a legitimate husband who can endow the foetus with spiritual life or a totemic soul they simply cannot become pregnant. Then too there are Italian women who are convinced that they were impregnated by a charismatic glance from Mussolini.

All these irrational beliefs show that in any rational human society, distinctions are made between the symbolic (irrational) systems devised by culture and the natural (rational) systems of the scientist. As far as 'virgin birth' is concerned, we are dealing with cultural beliefs about what is acquired from parents. Black Australians believe that a child receives its animal, physical substance from his mother, and only spiritual substance from its father. In aristocratic England 'blue' blood, symbol of lineage, came from the father, not from the mother. The idea of virgin birth involving physical substance from the mother and spirituality from the father should be comprehensible to westerners brought up in the christian magical tradition. There are cultures which do not 'believe in' physiological maternity; they hold that the foetus develops and grows entirely through the efforts of the husband-father. These people believe that a man's ejaculation projects a complete homunculus into the woman, his wife, and that it grows there, in a bag, until it is big enough to come out. Which primitive tribes could believe this? Our cultural ancestors, the ancient Greeks, denied that the woman played a significant physiological role in the development of the foetus; the mother merely went through the unrewarding wifely chore of bearing it.

White Australians in their innocence insist that the animal substance of a child comes from both parents and they ignore totemic spirits and clan souls. While the Black Australian father is concerned with the spiritual relationship between him and his child, the White Australian father fusses about the sperm that fertilizes his wife's ovum. His attitudes to the magic of conception and birth have been reduced to a very vulgar materialism. We believe in one child and two biological parents. The father in particular wants his child to be 'his' in a physical sense, and if he can prove that his wife's child is not 'his', he has the traditional moral and legal right to reject both of them. The White Australian male is more concerned with pride in his virility than with the joys of paternity, and Australian law is sometimes called upon to attempt to certify the paternity of a child. The church also supports this crudely biological view of the family: the act of sex is supposed to join a couple into eternal consubstantiality; husband and wife become 'one flesh' in christian beliefs. If a married couple does not consummate their union physically, their marriage is viewed by the church as null and void. A unique view of marriage indeed.

A Black Australian husband avoids delicate marital problems by ignoring the detail of biological paternity. He is not obsessed with his wife's sexual purity, as he prefers to stress the mystic and abstract forces which he controls in the child. Birth is a social event and most Aboriginal societies accept that children born to the wife belong to the husband. In Black Australia a husband could hardly demand his wife's sexual purity for their society has institutions such as wife-exchange and ritual orgies; also, adultery is commonplace in these communities where old men marry the majority of nubile young women. In White Australia on the other hand, a husband may even seek a divorce on the grounds that his wife became pregnant through artificial insemination (AID). Judges however are now frequently ruling that wives can use AID with or without the consent of impotent or sterile husbands.

The belief in virgin birth and spiritual rather than physical paternity offers some comfort to Black Australian men confronted with the overwhelming importance of women in the production of children. Only recently have White men woken up to a fact that their Black brothers have known for centuries: that the physical role of the father cannot compare in any way with nine months of pregnancy, the taboos and food prescriptions, the labour, the delivery, the breast-feeding, the joyous celebration of motherhood. The husband-father is a drone, impregnating the female and lying back to wait. Previously, when people blindly accepted the idea of the sacred christian family, women married because they had no choice: their sexual and maternal roles could not be satisfied outside holy matrimony. For hundreds of years we have 'believed' that for women to conceive legitimately they must be married to biological drones; unmarried women were under a ban and fatherless children were bastards.

Biology and sex create human babies but do not necessarily keep together families. Sex for Black Australians is an erotic pastime. They believe that semen enters the vagina, and then the uterus, and serves as an emulsion for the embryo to float on, 'like a water-lily on a pond'. The likeness between a father and his child is explained not by the facts of physical conception, but by the constant proximity of the man to his pregnant wife: his external presence moulds the child in the womb in his likeness. It is unnecessary to correct Black Australian ideas of paternity – they are statements about the soul and the spiritual make-up of their children. They are cultural, theological statements similar to the christian statement that Mary was a virgin when she conceived Jesus. White Australians and Black Australians who believe in virgin birth and immaculate conception are not ignorant of scientific information: they are discussing a different subject – the relationship between gods and men.

What is important about virgin birth is the social and mystical relationship between fathers and mothers, husbands and wives, parents and children through the cultural facts of birth, sex and marriage. This relationship involves the dual nature of human beings, physical and spiritual. Although this may be so, the comparison of Black Australian beliefs and the great christian myth of the virgin birth may be seen as forced. The term 'virgin birth' in the Black Australian case seems misplaced as all these virgin mothers enjoy copulation a couple dozen times a month throughout their reproductive lives. I agree that 'virgin' is perhaps the wrong term. But was the 'Virgin' Mary a virgin? In the Bible God not infrequently caused generation through his 'will' with the help of human copulation and physical impregnation; in many instances in the Old Testament there is the conviction or convention that the wife is a 'virgin'. Sarah, for example, became a 'young girl' – or virgin – again. A careful reading of Matthew 1:18 indicates that Joseph probably had intercourse with Mary during her pregnancy if not before. It could be that the child's conception took place in two essential stages: a spiritual pregnancy first and a physical or human pregnancy afterwards, the fruit being a single, miraculous birth. It is only the modern church which is committed to the exaggerated dogma that Mary was a virgin even when Jesus was born.

Father and child

Whatever the case, virgin birth is an interesting phenomenon wherever it occurs; in Black Australia the interest lies in its ubiquitousness – all births are virgin, all conceptions immaculate. Psychologists as well as theologians and anthropologists have puzzled over the ignorance – feigned or unfeigned – of physiological paternity. Black Australians insist on rejecting man's role in procreation and the psychoanalysts assume that they are unconsciously also rejecting their fathers and father-figures. Psychoanalysts maintain that, like many westerners, Blacks try to deny the father's sexual role. The father is an ambiguously loved and hated figure: loved as father, jealously hated as mother's husband. Children, resenting their father as their mother's sexual partner, have denied that he was their genitor. Blacks have supposedly turned this love–hate, fear–guilt syndrome into a general cultural rule which denies the father's role in conception through sexual intercourse; by denying this fact, Black Australians have resolved the Oedipus conflict which still haunts the west. Unfortunately a closer look at the facts fails to support this ethnocentric explanation. There is certainly no attempt to deny, hide or otherwise cover up the active sexual life between husband and wife from their children. By understanding the family and the complementary roles of father and mother, we put into correct perspective the Black Australian's belief in virgin birth. Black Australian husbands have exclusive rights over their wives and powerful rights over the children born to her. Paradoxically they maintain a powerful paternal role by ignoring the relatively insignificant physical role of the male in the birth of children and by maintaining that it is the husband who prepares the way for the spirit-child, and may even find the totemic spirit, that enters the wife's womb.

For the White Australian father, the biological drone, there are few customs which make him feel essential as father. Originally christian baptism emphasized the superiority of spiritual paternity over natural filiation. Baptism and god-parenthood involved a regeneration and a rebirth of spiritual life and theologians maintained a separation between natural and spiritual paternity. The natural father provided his child with mere corporeal substance; a spiritual father, the god-father who was once also the physical father, gave him the gift of grace.

From an anthropological point of view, a belief in virgin birth shows that in Black Australian society the relationship between a woman's child and a woman's husband stems from the recognition of the bonds of marriage, not the animal-like biological facts of sex. The husband – whether he is an impotent old man, a cuckold (or even a woman or a ghost in other societies) – is still the father of the child. The mother's role as procreator and giver of bodily life is stressed. Men credit women with the sole power to create flesh but claim for themselves the more important gift of creating spirit. Moreover Black beliefs avoid the awkward complications of male sterility and impotence.

A father has much to gain by being the 'godfather' rather than the physical genitor of his child. The child's relationship with his father is placed on a different, higher level than that with his mother. The father bestows rights to totemic lodges and hunting territory, and this control forges a strong link between father and child, particularly father and son, which is consolidated during the initiation rites when the son is symbolically reborn to his father. The father–son relation-ship in Black Australia is more intricate and more enduring than the same relationship in White Australia, where the father who claims undisputed biological paternity and no spiritual paternity, attends his wife's delivery, and rushes off to offer cigars to his mates and shares with them a barrel of beer.

The Black Australian's determination to assume full social paternity and to build permanent links of affection and moral responsibility with his children explains very clearly the supposedly mysterious institution of the couvade. The couvade, like many exotic institutions, at first sight has no logic. Why should a man feel morning sickness, undergo labour pains, and lie in bed exhausted after his wife has produced the child? The couvade reflects the fact that the birth of a child involves a change of status, a passage rite, for the husband as well as the wife. A young man becomes a husband, then a father, progressing from one position of status and responsibility to a higher one. The couvade provides symbolic behaviour to express this important transition; it also compensates in a way for the fact that the woman, not her husband, actually produces the child. The father shares his wife's food taboos and gives up his normal routine activities to accentuate his role as legitimate social father of the child born to his wife.

The Black father-to-be undertakes a series of actions that establish him as an important parent. When a woman becomes pregnant both she and her husband are warned by elders not to eat certain animals and plants; some of the taboos are shared, others are individual. As the woman's time approaches, the husband too feels birth pangs. Since some of the symptoms of genuine pregnancy can be assumed by women in false or hysterical pregnancies, and since many features of childbirth – such as a desire for special foods – may be cultural rather than physical demonstrations of the fact of being pregnant, there is no reason why fathers-to-be should not be sick in the mornings, avoid certain foods and make demands on others as an expression of their intimate participation in pregnancy.

In many ways the couvade functions in a way similar to the newly discovered – or invented – institution of male menopause in western societies: middle-aged husbands experience symptoms usually associated with physiological changes in the female. When the couvade is practised – and all societies (White Australians tend to be unaware of the symbolism of male, or female, morning sickness or food cravings) practise it to a greater or lesser extent – men are affirming an approaching status change, and symbolizing the transitional period of the passage rite of paternity; when the male menopause is experienced the hot flushes and nervous tensions are symbolic expressions of the passage of a young man into middle or old age.

The status of mother and the status of baby are easy to claim and celebrate. The making of a father is another matter. The doubts about paternity are approached by the White and Black father from two diametrically opposed directions: the former uses every means at his disposal to ensure that he and he alone is the physical progenitor of his wife's babies; the latter feels that the important thing is to be recognized as the spiritual progenitor of his wives' children. Unfortunately for the White Australian father, his role is being more and more undermined. In Black Australia the family, composed of two parents, socializes the child, nurtures it and endows it spiritually as well as teaching it basic male and female roles. In western countries the two-parent family is no longer the only type of family and many people argue that the one-parent family is more natural. It remains to be seen whether a trend for fatherless families will continue. In 1977 in Australia this trend was sanctified by capitalist enterprise in a national ceremony when the Baby Australia competition, run by Heinz, symbol of all that is wholesome and good in baby-care and family life, was won by a fatherless bastard.

In White Australia the male role in the family is in fact declining in importance, corresponding to the minimal biological role of the husband-father. Until recently he was needed to bring home the meat and the pay packet and to support the mother in raising the children. Now many women are doing it alone with the moral support of the state and public opinion. Even the influence of a nominal father-figure over his children is being steadily eroded by such factors as earlier school age, the radical increase in divorce, and legal provisions which almost automatically give custody of the children to their mother. Mothers are always given a superior right to the family home; she may sell it, take the children where she wishes and also claim a share of the husband's income. In some modern households the father's role has become little more than that of a nanny or surrogate mother, helping his wife in her maternal chores.

The Black Australian long ago recognized that law and biological chance are not enough to establish fatherhood. A father provides spiritually and materially for his child who in return provides for him at a later stage. Whether the father is biologically linked to his child is as irrelevant as the colour of his hair or the length of his big toe. The uselessness of the White Australian sperm mystique is shown by the frequent rejection of the father by young White Australians and the abandoning of old fathers by their prosperous middle-aged sons. The powerful ties engendered by spiritual fatherhood are shown by the love and affection given a Black Australian by his son in old age.

Part Two
Passage to Childhood

Chapter Three
At the Breast

The physical passage of birth and the cultural passage of naming are two milestones of early childhood. Black and White children begin to smile and crow, learn to crawl and walk and their achievements are appropriately marked and rewarded. Some of these milestones seem to be natural, instinctual; others have to be learned. Some are passed without fuss; others are celebrated. In some societies a child's first hair-cut is a momentous occasion celebrated by a community feast. In others it's his first teeth that call for a gathering. In White Australian society, teething is a time of stress for mother and child, not an occasion for joyful ceremony; but a few years later, when the teeth drop out, fairies visit and leave ritual gifts. Black Australians recognize weaning, at three or four years of age, with special rites; White Australians pay more attention to successful toilet-training. In Black Australian society, neither the coming nor going of the milk teeth involves rites, but later, one, or both, of the upper canines of both boys and girls is removed as part of the cultural process of growing up.

Of the innumerable critical passages of early childhood, I shall discuss only two – the two universal status passages of infancy – weaning and toilet-training. In both Black and White Australia they are recognized as important steps in maturation involving an initial separation from the mother. Weaning may be a violent, sudden affair at a few months (White Australia) or a slow gradual process tailing off after a number of years (Black Australia). Toilet-training too may be a violent and sudden affair (beginning at the age of a few months in White Australia) or a gradual process tailing off after several years (Black Australia). A comparison of the Black and White methods is of particular interest because both weaning and toilet-training are intricately and intimately involved with the five traditional human 'drives' stressed by psychologists: the oral (nursing, weaning, feeding), anal (toilet-training) drives, dependency and independence (involving the first two), and sexuality and aggression. As every anthropologist knows, particularly those who entertain psychological theories, the basis of culture and personality is acquired during the very early years: at the mother's breast and on the pottie, so to speak.

Early socialization

In making my ethnographical enquiries in small-town and urban Australia, I carefully checked on attitudes to breast-feeding, weaning, toilet-training and other associated aspects of baby-care and 'mothercraft'. These attitudes vary surprisingly, even in homogeneous White Australia. Traditional methods, acquired from mothers and grandmothers and old-fashioned nursing sisters are still used; but the younger generation apparently approaches time-tables and early toilet-training with a more relaxed attitude than the previous generation: Dr Spock reigns supreme.

I naturally wanted to know about the methods used when I was a baby because the generation which grew up in the 1930s and 1940s will now be showing the effects of the then current weaning and toilet-training methods. In the 1930s in Tasmania Truby King was the baby king and as an introduction to this chapter here is a quotation from the sacred text of his mothercraft book used by thousands, no millions, of Tasmanian, Australian and British mothers. The quotation refers to several important aspects of child-rearing which I shall be considering: the importance of breast-feeding, time-tables, the degree of body contact, attitudes to 'holding-out' or toilet-training, 'common sense' and 'natural laws' in the early socialization of the child.

A real Truby King baby . . . is one whose mother brings it up strictly according to the Truby King system – a baby who is completely breast fed till the ninth month and then weaned slowly on humanised milk, with a gradual introduction of solid foods as described in this book.

Truby King babies are fed four-hourly from birth, with few

exceptions, and they do not have any night feeds. A Truby King baby has as much fresh air and sunlight as possible, and his right amount of sleep. His education begins from the very first week, good habits being established which remain all his life.

A real Truby King baby is not too fat – every bit of his flesh is firm and clear. His eyes are bright, and one has only to hold him for a moment to appreciate his muscular tone. He is not treated as a plaything, made to laugh and crow and 'show off' to every visitor to please his parents' vanity; yet, he is the happiest thing alive, gambolling with his natural playthings, his own hands and toes; he is interested in the new and wonderful things which come within the range of his vision and touch, and is as full of abounding vitality as the puppy playing in the yard.

He sleeps and kicks out-of-doors as much as the weather allows, and sleeps at night in the airiest bedroom, or on an open verandah or porch, being carefully protected by a screen to keep him from draughts. After he has gone through his regular morning perform-ance of bathing and being 'held out', and has had his breakfast, he sleeps all the morning. If he wakes a little before his 2 p.m. meal, all one knows about it is a sudden-glimpsed chubby little leg and foot waved energetically from his cot for exercise or inspec-tion, or a vigorous jerking of his pram.

Altogether he is a joy from morning till night to himself and all the household – a perfectly happy and beautiful 'real Truby King baby'. The mother of such a baby is not overworked or worried, simply because she knows that by following the laws of nature, combined with common sense, baby will not do otherwise than thrive.*

Let us see how the Black mother, frequently maligned in the past, deals with bringing up baby. Valuing her baby highly, she indulges it in a very un-Truby King manner: White Australians call it 'spoiling', most other peoples call it 'mothering'. During the child's early years the mother sees her main job in life as one of constant care and protection of her child. She tries to make the child's upbringing a loving and easy-going affair prior to the traumatic moment of

*Sir F. Truby King, *Feeding and Caring for Baby*, 1925, by permission of Mac-millan, London and Basingstoke.

initiation for a boy, or early marriage for a girl. For the first
nine months or year the child is carried everywhere by the
mother, or one of his surrogate mothers, in a wooden trough
or a basket slung from her shoulders. After about a year the
child begins to ride on the mother's shoulders, clinging to
her head or hair. The child is always with relatives and never
left alone; if it cries the mother brings it immediately to the
comfort of the breast. She and her female kin lavish constant
affection on the child, blowing gently on its body, stroking
and cuddling it, and keeping up a steady flow of baby talk.
The child is never relegated to a 'nursery area' or left to play
with its toes but lives with the family; it is not sent away
when the parents indulge in sexual activities or squabble,
or when the elders discuss 'grown-up' business such as camp
affairs and ceremonies.

Truby King, of course, would consider the Black baby
spoiled and the Black mother a slave to the child's whims
and selfish greed for tender affection and body contact. If
a Black child does not get its own way, he may throw himself
on the ground in a screaming fit, writhing and kicking; everyone makes a desperate attempt to calm him, but if the tan-
trum continues the child is ignored except for an occasional
shout of exasperation. There is no concept of corporal punishment although a mother or father may occasionally slap
a child in hot blood. In fact the child is treated so leniently
that even if it picks up a spear and throws it at an adult or
pummels his mother violently nobody stops him. This
lenient attitude, this 'spoiling', is a common child-rearing
technique in many parts of the world. I doubt that in the
Aboriginal languages there is any single word which trans-
lates our word 'spoiling'. In Italy I am sometimes shocked
at what loving parents let their children do. Yet there must
be reason in the madness of Black Australian and Italian
indulgent parents since these wild, unruly, overpetted children do succeed in becoming sane, intelligent, normal adults.
Black children are controlled, of course – not through punishment but through precept: their elders tell them moral
tales around the camp-fire, tales of evil spirits and ogres and
the bunyip; a child who shows off continually soon gets

called a 'big-head' and is shamed by ridicule into conformity.

White Australian children are dependent on their parents and have formal ties with them until the age of eighteen when many leave home with a sigh of relief and return for the occasional Christmas or funeral. What went wrong? Whose fault is it, mother's, father's or child's? Unlike the Black Australian, the 'traditional' White Australian father is often a negative figure in the domestic world. He goes to work and digs the garden to keep out of the way of his wife and children; he fantasizes by the trout stream, in the garden shed or in the make-believe world of mates and beer, but at home the mother rules supreme. The mother is the moral guardian, source of love, goddess of a mythical world of seductive cakes and floral curtains in the lounge. The mother controls the home. She even mocks the father who is not always a shining example of mature manhood and on the whole her sons turn to their mother who discharges her love on them all. But what a love: the soft maternal mother also thrashes her children with a spiky hair-brush, so that they soon learn that love and discipline come from the same source. Fear and love are a dreadful combination and the inevitable revolt imposes a terrible guilt; the child has learned to associate morals, right and love with femininity, and immorality, wrong and often fear with masculinity, because father must carry out the threats mother uses, 'Wait till your father hears what you've done – then you'll get it.'

Motherhood for Black Australian women seems to be a serene, if full-time affair. Despite the business and hardship of the nomadic life, her babies are the centre of her life; the relationship between mother and child is the most intense, the most lasting of all relationships based on love, marriage or friendship. Motherhood is hardly a serene affair for White Australian women, haggard from sleepless nights, looking after screaming babies alone, struggling to bring up babies in the isolation of a suburban house or urban flat, with the reluctant help of their husbands. White Australian motherhood is not all maternal joy and contentment, but a constant neurotic swing between love for the child and resentment at the loss of her independence and peace of mind. For the

Black mother and child, the relationship is relaxed and enduring; for White Australians it seems to be a source of neurosis for both mother and child and of bemusement for the father.

I think for many White Australian women it is the isolation in the famous nuclear family that makes motherhood a harrowing as well as rewarding experience. A woman has her baby in hospital where she and the baby are cared for by a host of starched servants. Then lo! the moment she gets out of the hospital wheelchair and is helped into the taxi by her husband, she is handed baby and motherhood – all of it – and she must go home to an empty house and cope by herself. White Australian women bring up their children alone, unless you count the emerging mothering father; she learns to be proud of the fact that she is the only caretaker, the only nurturant, the only breast and the only consolation available to the child.

Black mothers and their babies are not trapped in the closed world of the nuclear family, but have strong personal relationships with many other members of the local community who are 'mothers', 'grandmothers', 'aunts', 'mothers-in-law'. For a stranger in a Black Australian camp it may be difficult to distinguish by behaviour alone which is the natural mother since the children are constantly cuddled and caressed and suckled by many different people. The White mother devotes herself to her child often without the help of aunts and grandmothers whom she usually rejects in a no uncertain manner. The mother becomes a domestic dictator, sacrificing herself for her children. While being the sole, overwhelming nurturant, she unconsciously resents her time-consuming children and wreaks a violent revenge on them with severe weaning practices, strict feeding times and an almost sadistic toilet-training scheme.

Many mothers, arriving home from hospital, are actually frightened of their first child; without any previous experience and without the help and guidance of older relatives they do not know what to do. Young Black women on the other hand have ample opportunity to see other mothers caring for their children and although a first child may be treated a little awkwardly, the basic experience is there. The point is that matrescence, including maternal love, is not natural, instinctual behaviour but is part of learned, imitated behaviour. Even among man's closest animal relatives the maternal drive is not purely instinctive; learning and precept encourage young females to acquire 'maternal love'. Among primates in the wild the maternal experience is shared, as it is among Black Australians: a new-born infant and its mother become a focus of attention for other female members of the troop and the infant is held by aunts and nieces and young female cousins in turn. Among langurs, for example, this sharing of the maternal role is very obvious: within a few hours of birth the baby is handed around to other members of the troop. In zoos, when chimpanzees and gorillas are raised in isolation, they have no opportunities to learn about motherhood and they sometimes reject or even destroy their babies. White Australian mothers in their cages have Truby King or Dr Spock.

One of the basic facts of child-care is that children need constant attention, particularly lots of body contact. Yet Truby King advises that children spend long hours in quiet rooms, playing with hands and toes, instead of being with parents and their friends. As a result, in White Australia where they are at least fed well, babies rarely cry from hunger: they cry from loneliness because of having been left alone in distant nurseries or on back verandahs. New-born babies are programmed to cling to their mother's body and stay there. It has been shown that most non-human mammals could not survive without this close physical relationship with their mother which sustains them in the defenceless early period. For at least three months the rhesus macaque mother cradles, supports, grooms her child and will not leave it on its own for a moment. During the period when the White Australian baby is forced to be independent in its cot, the rhesus macaque baby clings to its mother; it even has a differently coloured coat from adults which indicates its special status as a helpless, dependent, clinging baby and which diverts adult aggression and sexuality.

The Black child too is constantly held and caressed; it

suckles when hungry and sleeps with its mother, remaining, as nature seems to have intended, to all intents and purposes, physically part of her for the first months. All babies need this body contact, this receptiveness, softness and motherly smell as soon as the cord is cut. If there is an enforced separation, the mother–child bond is imperfectly formed and the child suffers deprivation. In Africa, when hunters killed monkeys with babies the infants were brought to me; separated from their mothers they developed the rocking, crouching movements of deprived children in western culture. The mothers also need to feel and smell their babies after birth; otherwise, like animals who do not immediately find and suckle their babies after birth, they may reject them.

We are aware of these basic animal facts yet we do not learn from them. In many hospitals in Australia, America and Europe, once the baby is born it is taken away from the mother so that she is not disturbed; frequently drugged, she often sleeps for several hours instead of immediately relating to the baby in a close physical fashion. And the baby, instead of clinging to its mother, is taken into a harshly lit nursery, handled by strangers in cold, starched uniforms, labelled so that its mother can recognize it and given an artificial teat to stop it from crying. Even before the afterbirth is expelled, the baby is put in a room apart from the mother; two sets of people look after two separate individuals, the mother and the child. Fortunately, new developments, such as the Leboyer method and birth centres, are revolutionizing the mother–child relationship, particularly in America.

In hospital the mother is treated as an invalid and is looked after by doctors and nurses and not allowed to perform her natural role. The art of mothering is difficult enough to learn without eliminating those instinctual elements associated with close physical contact. Studies of the important role of mother–child tactile stimulation have been made with chickens, cats, sheep and dolphins, and evidence indicates that animals that are handled from the moment of birth grow up practically unfearful in situations of stress and show no unnatural aggression. Baby rats are much happier baby rats if they are kept close to their mothers or even constantly handled by humans. Removing a baby rat from its home cage and placing it in an isolated box – like taking a baby from its mother after birth and placing it in a brightly lit nursery – produces lasting deleterious effects. Other experiments approximating the effects of modern techniques of child-birth and post-natal care – such as exposure to sudden shock or sudden cold – result in life-long anxiety. Yet we do not think it unnatural to remove the baby from the warmth and comfortable darkness of the womb and put it in a box in a glassed-in, light-filled room.

One friend of mine said that her first baby was not brought to her until fifteen hours after it was born. The hospital routine was to bring all new-born babies to their mothers first thing in the morning, so that if the mother delivered in the late morning she had to wait almost twenty-four hours to see her baby. This story once again highlights the reason behind many of the odd practices involved in modern child-care: it is not ignorance or cruelty that causes the separation of child from mother but convenience. Much of the progress' in birth techniques and baby-rearing stems from a desire to make life easier for gynaecologist, nurse and mother. But efficiency and convenience, of course, are not necessarily the answers to human problems. It should be obvious that for the well-being of the child, for good parent–infant relations, and for a sane adulthood, White Australian babies, like Black babies, should remain in close contact with their mothers so that they can be physically stimulated according to fundamental biological laws. Convenience as we have seen is responsible for the dramatic increase in Caesarean surgery which also involves an unnatural separation of mother and child; the children tend to be anxious, shy and have more behavioural problems than babies born by the more natural, mammalian methods. Convenience means less and less body contact, more and more time-tables and results in a situation in which, like uncoddled rats, many White Australians, myself included, remain aggressive in stressful situations and are unable to cope comfortably in complex civilized life.

Black baby is king for three or four years, until he is weaned and toilet-trained. White Baby is king for less than a year, knocked off his paper throne at weaning, when his mother introduces the bottle because she is going back to work, or hands over the breast to the next baby or to her husband. White babies are brought up in ways to suit the mother's life style – many mothers are out at work, and even a middle-class housewife has many other things to do beside providing constant body-contact – bridge parties, tennis parties, church work, flower arrangements, choir practice, country women's meetings. In Black Australia baby comes first; in White Australia mother comes first. And this basic difference is reflected perhaps most dramatically in the Black and White attitudes to breast-feeding and weaning.

Breast-feeding and weaning

Attitudes to breast-feeding and weaning have been studied and compared in countless human and animal societies. Like the human baby, the new-born primate infant is totally dependent on its mother; she nurtures him physically and emotionally. In a few species of primates, such as African savannah baboons, the infant is rejected when the mother re-enters the reproductive cycle with her first post-partum oestrus (heat). Most often, however, weaning is not completed before the next pregnancy and is sometimes delayed till after the birth of the new infant. Lactation does not occur after the mother re-enters the oestrus cycle, but the infant is still carried and permitted to suckle the nipple for comfort – a kind of security thumb-sucking or blanket-clutching rather than a means of nourishment. Among most primates weaning is not a sudden and traumatic rejection. Chimpanzee babies drink every ninety minutes or so up till the age of a year and a half, but they are allowed to drink more often; when they go on short forays in the bush, they keep coming back to the mother to seek comfort at the breast. When the infant is about three and a half, the mother usually conceives again and the baby is weaned.

Weaning among sub-human primates, then, occurs at a time when the child has learned to leave the mother and to explore wider social relationships, while maintaining some ties with the mother. The baby chimpanzee turns to its peer group for interaction and begins to sleep apart from the mother. Among Black Australians and most human societies apart from our own there is a similar pattern. Weaning occurs when the child stops being a baby and begins to walk and talk, when he is beginning to be a rational member of society. Weaning is treated as a passage rite among Black Australians, because it is the time when the child should begin to become independent of its mother, like the chimpanzee child; it should be remembered however that there is evidence that the physical tie between mother and child is never completely severed while both are alive.

The situation of the 'civilized' baby is indeed anomalous, if not unnatural. I was weaned in Truby King fashion on 13 September, nine precise months after birth. Today babies are weaned earlier for various reasons: the mother goes back to work, she wants to keep her breasts firm, or she fears that the resumption of sex (an unfounded fear) and the use of the Pill will cause her milk to dry up. Weaning among White Australians cannot provide a ritual transition from helpless babyhood to semi-independent childhood. Black Australians separate the child from the mother when it begins to talk and 'to stand on its own feet' by introducing it to new kinds of adult food – often white-coloured paps reminiscent of breast milk. White Australian infants do not have a ritual separation from the mother at the age of three or four, because they have been weaned at six or nine months, unless the unspectacular moment of being left at kindergarten is such a ceremony. In many ways the White Australian mother does not cease playing an exaggerated maternal role until her children are much older, using baby talk and baby food to maintain an iron-like grip on them. This is a dangerously ambivalent attitude: the mother, while denying the child her physical body at a very early age, is unwilling or unable to let her children move into the world of their agemates.

The most important element in mother–baby contact is the breast. There is much more to breast-feeding than nutrition and feeding, much more than the tactile stimulation to a child's lips which comes from suckling. With breast-feeding the baby's face comes into contact with the warmth and smoothness of the mother's skin; this contact provides the child with human comfort that has great psychological and symbolic importance. The relationship between a mother and her baby at her breast provides the model for all sane relationships formed later in the child's life – relationships involving trust, love, giving and receiving. The word for son in Latin, *filius*, is derived from the word for sucking the breast, the word for daughter in English from the word milk.

It goes without saying that all Black mothers suckle their children; observers have found no examples of women who have no milk or babies who refuse to suck. The only babies I have come across who were incapable of suckling were mentally deficient or infants born with cleft palates, and, in Black Australia, these would have been killed at birth because it is clear they could not survive in a hunting and gathering community. Babies are breast-fed by both their mothers and their surrogate mothers.

Black Australians believe, rightly, that the breast is essential to the happiness and normalcy of a child until weaning at the age of three or four. It is acknowledged that the baby needs emotional and physical contact with its mother until he is weaned, without competition or interference from a younger child. It is wrong to believe that babies are spaced out in primitive society because mothers have only a limited supply of milk. On the contrary, mother surrogates are always available. What the child requires is not only nutrition but maternal affection associated with physical contact. Understanding this need explains the unusual custom whereby if another baby is born before a child is weaned, the older child has the right to take the breast away from the younger who may become weakened as a result. It also throws light on the traditional practice of killing a second child born too soon after the first; Black Australians feel that the mother cannot provide sufficient maternal care for both children and infanticide is considered imperative. I was conceived five months after my brother was born; I was not smothered at birth but was allowed to take over the breast and my mother's complete attention when my brother was only fourteen months old.

On the whole, White women who do breast-feed their babies do so for very short, inadequate periods. Unlike Black mothers who do not insist on a convenient nursing schedule but allow their babies to suck at any time of the day or night, White mothers follow a time-table and usually wean their babies before a year is up. Nevertheless these women believe they are giving their babies a good start in life from both a psychological and physiological point of view. Bottle-feeding, of course, is more convenient and can be carried out by the husband or another surrogate mother. Yet there must be more important reasons why children are fed artificially in the west since few mothers are unaware of the higher incidence of problems involving bone formation, tooth development and psychological adjustment among bottle-fed babies. An important reason is that bottle-feeding leaves the mother's breast firm and attractive for her husband; the mother sacrifices her maternal role to her wifely sexual role. In this case, the sex life of husband and wife competes with the complete mother–child relationship. In the west, the more demanding the baby is of the mother, the more the husband feels shut out and jealous, shut out not only from the relationship between mother and child, but also from his relationship with his wife. Some husbands demand equal or more attention. Others accept the maternal role as surrogate mother, sublimating jealousy by sharing the joys and responsibilities of motherhood.

Sex between a Black mother and her husband does not create this problem particularly if the family is a polygynous one. The taboo on sex after the birth of a child may last from a year to up to three or four years or until weaning. The post-natal sex taboos are accompanied by widely held beliefs – also found among White Australians – that copulation harms the breast milk and hence the baby, and that while a baby is being breast-fed the mother will not conceive. A taboo on sex between husband and wife, mother and father, means that in the early months and years of a baby's life, a woman's love is given exclusively to her baby. No Black mother would dream of not giving her full attention to her baby and its emotional demands because her husband showed signs of feeling neglected; she would simply advise him to take another wife or to find sex elsewhere.

The sexual taboo imposed by White doctors is of the 'hygienic' variety and may last only a few weeks. White husbands, and even wives, seem more interested in their own sexual satisfaction than in their parental roles or the psychological state of their children. Babies are put in the unusual position of having to compete with their mother's husband for affection and even for the breast itself! It is for the sake of the husband and sex that White Australian babies are ripped untimely from the breast. For this reason babies who are weaned at an excessively early age need dummies, cuddly toys and blankets to replace the mother who has gone back to her husband's bed.

Infantilism

The breast should be recognized not only as a source of food but also as a source of comfort. In African societies children are allowed to find comfort by playing with the mother's breast till the age of six or seven even if she no longer has any milk. The reason for the breast being a source of infantile consolation is not hard to find: the mother provides food, the mother provides protection and the breast comes to symbolize both food and security. Artificial feeding, of course, divests the breast of its symbolic function particularly when it is turned into a fetish and covered with several layers of clothing. A human child runs to the breast when frightened, in the same way as does a chimpanzee; a half-grown kangaroo too will run to his mother and hide his head in her pouch. White Australians brought up on bottles and little bodily contact have no source of comfort unless it is the mother's skirts, or the bottle.

The denial of the breast as a normal source of food and of security leaves many White Australian adults with a psychological complex. White Australians have a short suckling period and are reassured with relatively little cuddling and grooming; breasts are hidden and attributed excessively erotic significance. Black Australians have a long suckling period, and are accustomed to uncovered breasts and a good deal of interpersonal body contact. For Black Australians breasts are not inflammable erogenous zones. White males often vaunt the fact that they have fetishes about breasts and believe that their feelings are part of universal virile sexuality. In reality, the great, buxom breast of the ubiquitous pin-up is not a sign of adult sexuality but of infantilism and maternal deprivation. These ladies are not sex-symbols – they are mother-symbols. For this reason some men buy cars advertised with bosomy ladies seated on the bonnet or inside; they fall heavily for the big-breasted maternal type of girl; they cover the walls of their rooms with naked breasts.

This breast-symbolized infantilism is a phenomenon found throughout the so-called civilized world. White Australians grow up and pass exams and win athletic and swimming races and learn skills, but without the accompanying emotional maturity. Is it going too far to suggest that this emotional immaturity began in early childhood when the child was precociously deprived of breast satisfaction? Westerners, toilet-trained and weaned far too early, refuse to grow up, refuse to enter a normal life-cycle. Most observers have placed the blame firmly on their mothers, women who lavish their creative energies and frustrated sexuality on their sons, refusing them the breast but overwhelming them with chocolate-layer cakes and exotic milk puddings. No ceremonies, no rites, no exigencies of work or even sexual desire seem to be able to tear them from the mother-dominated world.

The moment the anthropologist begins his field work among White Australians, he is confronted with examples of infantilism. Advertisements flaunt the maternal breast, people pet in public; their odd diet of children's food is supplemented by a new sexual diet of massage, bondage and sucking. Women have a passion for sweet, cute baby-like things and people, for pets with round, soft, baby-like looks of Disney's Bambi or the koala. Exaggerated infantile characteristics call forth the frustrated instincts of women who have denied themselves the complete joys of maternity. At the cinema they prefer stars with baby looks; at elections they often vote for clean-shaven boyish politicians – as American women elected Kennedy and Carter.

Now infantilism can be attractive. Everyone loves the cheery, brown, youthful charm of the American and Australian in the prime of life. And infantilism to some degree is found in all people and even animals. A bird may beg ('gape') like a baby bird if he finds himself in a difficult situation. Infantile behaviour in animals is often an imitation of female behaviour; it prevents aggression by making high-ranking males think the supposed challengers are 'babies' and need fatherly treatment. Some animals get stuck in infantility. Young stags which are sexually mature, but have high-ranking males above them, fail to mate successfully and often show no inclination to do so. Some birds – cattle egrets are an example – prefer to 'marry' their mothers so they can go on being fed as babies. In captivity their dependency can last a long time; in the wild, the parents stay away from the nest to encourage the grown-up bird to get out, grow up, find a mate and seek its own prey.

In Australia, I noticed an exaggerated degree of infantilism in the clothes, food, language, even marriage patterns of White Australians. One of the first things that struck me is the degree to which Australian families are child-oriented. Everything revolves around the children: the meals, the holidays, the outings. In Africa, where children are 'spoiled', family life is adult-oriented and the child is expected to fit in with adult activities once he is weaned. In Italy, children stay up till midnight and eat adult food at adult dinner parties. In Australia, even when there are guests, the evening meal may be served at five o'clock to cater for the children.

And when you sit down to eat, the food may well be children's food. In other parts of the world there is a distinction between what is good for children and what is good for adults. Black Australian children eat certain insects, snakes, plants which adults shun as 'baby food'. Food has symbolic value: its shape and colour indicate a variety of things and send a variety of messages. In western societies growing up should mean giving up babyish food along with the breast, milky puddings, sweets. Milk, for example, is ideal food for babies and calves, but most unnatural for grown-ups. Babies produce naturally an enzyme known as lactase which allows them to digest the milk-sugar lactose of mother's milk. When people stop suckling they stop producing this enzyme. I have never seen an African drink a glass of milk and there are certainly no milk-bars in Italy. Yet grown-up Australians remain addicted to milk and milky food, and to sweet, sugary food. I have seen a father of four go to work with a bottle of milk, a raspberry jam sandwich and a slice of cake left over from the women's sewing meeting. In the evening he comes homes to sausages and mashed potatoes, a vegemite sandwich, a glass of milk and a piece of pavlova cake left over from the afternoon bridge tea.

Food panders to childishness. The American and Australian milk-bar is a haven for infantile adolescents. There is an international industry in food for baby grown-ups which has no food value: the value is purely symbolic. Beer in Australia is the sweetest and the strongest in the world; and now that we know that hops have an overdose of female hormones we understand the double symbolism of the Australian national drink: infantile desires and feminine urges.

Like cattle egrets, Australian men often find it convenient to 'marry' their mothers, rather than becoming adult and independent. The woman in the average White Australian man's life is a maternal figure; when we are small, mummy cooks for us and washes our clothes; when we become big boys, our wives are expected to do the same. When we are small, we try to cuddle our mothers and when we are big we snuggle up to our wives. We even call them 'mum'. Sometimes when we wake up in the middle of the night after a bad dream we stretch out a frightened hand and call for mummy. By marrying his mother, the grown-up boy happily hands over all household arrangements and the entire domestic sphere to the wife-mother, and begins to act like her eldest son, spending most of the time with the boys or out playing. The little woman provides security and mothering and infantile food while the boy goes off in his shorts and long socks; she waits patiently for him to come home, fills him with cakes, washes his dirty clothes and puts him to bed with a scolding.

Australian dialects reflect these social patterns. White Australians have a remarkable line of adult baby-talk which makes learning the language, even for English-speakers, a rather trying business. Personal names are contracted into cuddly sounds: I am never Robert but Robbie, Rob, Bob, Bert, Bertie, even Ro. Everyday language is spiced with infantile expressions; 'o' is used constantly as an ending – smoko, milko, salvo, homo, reffo, arvo; and there are other abbreviations such as Aussie and Pommy, Woolies and Commy. If someone goes away with a romantic weekend with the postman's wife, he is having a 'naughty'. People don't take a hot-water bottle to bed; they take a hottie. Australians have brekkie not breakfast, a bikkie not a biscuit, Chrissie not Christmas, din-dins not dinner and vegies not vegetables. The game becomes difficult when you are faced with such arcane abbreviations as picky (picnic), blowy (blow fly) or mushy (mushroom).

Am I exaggerating? I don't think so: my professional opinion is backed up by personal experience. While it may seem hard-hearted to blame a nation's failing on the mothers and particularly on early child-care, the performance of White Australian mothers – those overwhelming matriarchs or cute little girls – is poor indeed compared to that of their Black sisters. Black children, while loving their mothers, show them no special respect or sentimental affection and frequently disobey and even abuse them, and it is very difficult for a White Australian woman to understand the Black mother's success in producing sons and daughters who grow up into singularly pleasant, relaxed and adult people. Black Australians seem calm and free of anxiety while Whites are often asthmatic, restless and filled with guilt. Most observers feel that the successful Black personality results from the strength and depth of the mother–child tie and from admirable early training methods; Black Australians have a serene personality that is rooted in the security given them by their mothers, a security begun at the breast.

Chapter Four

Excreta, Time and Property

Toilet-training

Attitudes to toilet-training follow the same pattern as attitudes to breast-feeding. On the whole White babies are toilet-trained according to rigid schedules while Black babies are permissively trained. White Australians, from an amazingly early age, learn that excrement is nasty and offensive and that it is best for all concerned if they defecate in certain places and at certain times. Black Australians have a more relaxed attitude; the principle behind toilet-training is the same as the one behind learning the language or the facts of family relationship: the activity, in this case defecating, is a natural process and the emphasis is mainly on imitation and example from older children and adults. If early weaning or prolonged breast-feeding can have such profound effects on the human psyche, there must too be results from precocious or tardy toilet-training. White parents aggressively teach their children to hold back their faeces and urine in order to learn self-control; but in learning control, White Australians often suffer psychic disturbances and life-long obsessions with the substances involved – urine and excrement – which affect their whole outlook on life.

All human beings, of course, must learn to defecate in the right place and at the right time, and to keep themselves clean afterwards. This universal human learning process is the result of the physical evolution of man. *Homo sapiens*, when he came down from the trees, gradually adopted an upright posture and a striding gait, and he also began to eat all kinds of food including meat. These changes led to the necessity of having to clean his anus after defecation. If it was left dirty, particularly in tropical areas where flies proliferate, life would be unbearably uncomfortable. For this reason all humans, but not all primates, learn to bring their excretory processes under control.

Toilet-training is usually initiated by the mother who instils the idea that faeces and urine are dirty things. To many anthropologists, the various ways of instilling this 'idea' are as interesting as the different ways of weaning children because of the consequences the methods have on the personality of adults in society. Primary attention has been paid to 'when' and 'how': at what age and by what means.

In White Australia, the emphasis has traditionally been on 'when'. 'When' is usually as early as possible – to fit in with the other household 'time-tables', to please the mother and for the 'convenience' of everyone concerned. The history of my own experience, recounted with pleased confidence by my mother and elder sisters, sounds outrageous to me now. Truby King (and consequently my female care-takers) had very precise ideas about toilet-training; he claimed that a well-organized, efficient mother could train a baby as young as a few weeks if it was regularly 'caught' at the right time and a habit made of it. To instil the habit, my mother and thousands of other Truby King mothers, placed a porcelain chamber-pot on her knees, and held the baby (me) over it after the morning feed so that I should feel, with a shock, the cold edge and learn to recognize that as a signal for defecating. If this did not work at once Truby King suggested that my mother gently stroke my anus with her finger: this intimate action – the stroking of the perineal region before defecation – is also a trigger for excretion among non-human mammals. Truby King mothers are advised to make a straining noise at the back of their throat at the same time, and the good little three-week-old baby was supposed to imitate it.

It has become, for some reason, of the utmost importance for a White mother to toilet-train her child as soon as possible; she therefore spends her time running after it with an icy pottie to catch it before it 'does it'. Many women become involved almost psychotically with this anal theme and are filled with abnormal pride at baby's success, or are overly-irritated if it dirties a new napkin or diaper. In this way, a natural process, defecating, and a cultural process, keeping the anus clean, become frightening ones because the extreme reactions of the mother are communicated to the child and can trouble him later.

Black toilet-training, on the other hand, is not based on the premises of needing to please mother and making life easier for her. The final successful regulation is postponed until the child can make decisions on its own; this usually happens at about the same time he is weaned, when he has begun to play with age-mates and walk by himself. Learning to control orifices does not involve constant and aggressive teaching in Black Australian societies. Adults, for example, show no concern, no mock horror when a small child urinates or defecates on them. Even toddlers can expect to have someone around to attend to them without any admonishment or feelings of shame and guilt. Like weaning, the ability to defecate outside the camp, cover it and keep his bottom clean is a passage rite that raises the child's status in the community; he becomes a clean child in a community of his peers, not a dirty baby in a world of babies. I found the same situation in Africa. I know of no societies other than western ones where mothers oblige children to sit on the toilet every morning at a certain time and let them out only when they have done their 'job'.

Learning to defecate also entails learning the culturally accepted position for defecation. White Australians sit, Black Australians squat. To urinate, White men stand and White women – imprisoned by their pants and skirts rather than their biology – sit. Black men on the other hand sit to urinate if they are sub-incised while some women stand.

Some of these facts, although they vary from culture to culture, are really unimportant; of greater interest are the attitudes to the action and substance of body elimination. Just as premature weaning can produce breast fixation in White Australians, traumatic toilet-training can and does result in a spectacular anal fixation. If control of bodily functions is taught extraordinarily early and in an abnormally aggressive manner, faeces and the anus often become fetishes in the same way that the tabooed, covered-up breast becomes a fetish. The sacred, polluting nature of body products and orifices is hidden away in euphemisms and the good little White Australian learns to deny his anus and its momentous activities. In fact most of them never rediscover it until they come across such 'obscenities' as enemas, anal suppositories and, when they go abroad, bidets. For a European it is hard to understand an Australian's attitude to the innocent bidet which has gained such an evil reputation in Australia through its association with the alleged sexual specialization of decadent continentals.

White Australians euphemistically refer to their basic functions as a 'call to nature', 'number one and number two'; they 'excuse themselves' and 'go to the bathroom' when they defecate. White Australians also avoid speaking of the anus as such and couch references in terms like 'derriere', 'posterior', 'bum', 'backside', and the spot is camouflaged with trouser pockets, long jackets and sweaters.

Pollutants

Harsh toilet-training and taboo attitudes inculcate a magical attitude to the anus and the urethra and their polluting products. Not only are these organs and basic human activities of elimination lewd and disgusting to White Australians, but, by extension, so are the sex organs because they are, as in most animals, intimately associated with excretory processes (as Yeats wrote, 'love has pitched his mansion in the place of excrement'). And from the sexual organs the filth and pollution is extended, even less logically, to other body orifices and their products. White Australians, I know from personal experience and from comparing my own delicate attitudes with those of non-Australian friends, have amazingly strong body-aperture taboos. As children we are taught not to burp, fart, pick our nose or teeth, yawn or sneeze in public. It is not only a matter of health consideration for others in crowded places, but a positive protection of orifices and their substances. White Australians prefer to put polluting mouth and nose excreta in a clean cloth in their pockets, instead of spitting and hawking away from their bodies like sensible Blacks. I have watched fascinated while a hygienic

White Australian removed a piece of bone, fat or gristle from his polluting mouth, covering the aperture and the substance with his hands, and hiding the contaminated and contaminating object under a convenient lettuce leaf.

The entrances to our body *are* dangerous and polluting, as are the substances that come out. This is one of the reasons why Black Australians do not kiss mouth-to-mouth. White Australians indulge in French kissing but are horrified of saliva as such once it has left the mouth; many people even refuse to drink from the same glass as a close friend or relative because of this irrational fear. It is for this reason we hide our body products in handkerchiefs and bathrooms, and shelter our orifices with special clothes, lipsticks, earrings, hairstyles and conventional gestures. We even extend our obsession with dangerous holes to our houses and gardens, trailing vines over porches, building porches over doors, curtaining and 'blinding' windows and putting a hedge around the back door.

Of course these magical attitudes to orifices of the body and their products are not unique to Australians, Americans and Europeans. All people have special, cultural attitudes to the body and have elaborated ways and means of avoiding the filthy excretions such as sweat, saliva, urine, menstrual blood and sexual fluids; yet in some cases the 'filthy excretion' may be converted into a benevolent substance. Among Black Australians, and probably among most cultural groups in the world, menstrual blood is often considered dangerous – an impurity which can make healthy people sick; at other times it has the magical power of curing disease. Other products also have positive value: breath may be 'bad' or positively benevolent in certain rituals. While sweat may be used in witchcraft as a harmful substance against enemies, it is also smeared on children by their parents in welcome and farewell.

The point is that for Black Australians the symbolic value of body excretions depends on the circumstances; White Australians are obsessed with filth as such. We believe in magical 'germ power': we have a fantasy, created by quack science, that each person has his own unique species of germs which must not be confused with anyone else's. Genuine science can show that millions of germs inhabit every healthy body but we prefer to regard them as trespassers and try to keep them off by an expensive and relentless struggle against dirt learned at our mother's knee and at the pottie. We believe that body products – even if they have disappeared from the place where they dropped or from the place where they might have dropped – leave an invisible, dreadful trace similar to the polluting substances described by precepts of the Hindu religion. We have a horror of the contaminating power of the invisible saliva on someone else's glass, the sweat on someone else's clothes, the non-existent signs of sex on the sheets and the invisible excrement on the toilet seat.

This obsession with the polluting nature of these substances is very closely tied to the aggressive toilet-training practices that are part of our upbringing. The White Australian philosophies of dirt and of hygiene are, in large part, derived from the toilet complex. We learn very early that faeces are polluting and should be hidden out of sight and not talked about. These ideas influence the way White Australians think. The word 'shit' is used to describe not only faeces, but also old people, homosexuals, the insane, and prisoners. Ideas about the institutionalization of the aged and the mad, the retarded and the sick are based on a lavatorial pattern of thought: the idea is that unwanted matter will disappear if it is removed from our field of vision. Our ideas of dirt are derived from our ideas about toilet-training and contribute to a system of categorization that is peculiar to the western world. To some 'rational' inhabitants of the civilized world, marginal persons are like marginal things (shit, snot, menstrual blood) – threatening and filthy because they can not be fitted into a neat framework. Australian newspapers often present prostitutes and transvestites, drunks and the deformed, even university students, as threatening or weird, odd or even dirty. The racist philosophy of the White Australia policy was based on these common attitudes to body elimination: I was taught to fear that the sluice-gates would open and we would drown in the shit of the Yellow Peril. Quaint, dirty, inconvenient old people are sometimes housed in shacks at the bottom of the garden where the toilet used to be and where dogs are kept; the mad are kept in asylums; homosexuals and New Australians form ghettos; Black Australians are put on reservations. When things do go wrong, and clean-living people are forced to take notice of the 'rising tide of filth' the right-wing newspapers claim we are drowning in, it is as though the septic tank has been blocked or the 'night man' has not come. Shocked and disgusted, holding our noses, we call on the government and the police – emergency plumbers – to put the matter right and hide it again.

Deprived of the breast as a child, the White Australian makes a fetish of it; deprived of the anus and his excrement, he makes a fetish of both of them. There is clearly an ambivalent attitude to excrement: the 'horror' is often accompanied by a positive fascination. Australian men in particular have dreadful doubts about the security of their orifices; this insecurity reaches an extreme form in 'normal' males in their obsessional fear of homosexuality and, in psychotics, of their being buggered. Women are less neurotic about their orifices, probably because they have become more used to natural body functions through their dealings with children, and because it is natural for them to be intruded sexually. While Australians treat orifices and body excretions with secret dread, there is no theme more delightful to them than the lavatorial theme. Best-selling books reveal this odd fascination, and as an Australian comic pointed out, 'If everything else fails just leave the stage and come back with a chamberpot on your head and you'll have them rolling in the aisles.' These ambivalent attitudes come out in jokes and horseplay, bawdy songs, and films such as *Don's Party* and the Barry McKenzie series, where deep taboos are given a deep and hilarious release. The favourite subjects are always vomiting, pissing, shitting, farting and buggery.

Bathrooms

This ambivalent attitude to the orifices and their substances may also explain why the civilized world deposits filthy excrement and other bodily excretions in marble halls, in elaborate suburban bathrooms. Black Australians observe the more normal custom of simply leaving the domestic zone, the camp, and covering their faeces with sand. This is the method advised in the Bible: we are told 'to have a place also without the camp whither thou shalt go forth abroad; and thou shalt have a paddle upon thy weapon; and it shall be when thou wilt ease thyself abroad, thou shalt dig therewith, and shall turn back and cover that which cometh from thee' (Deuteronomy 23:12 and 13). Perhaps for the Ancient Hebrews, as for Black Australians, the motives behind covering up excrement were more religious than hygienic: Black Australians hide it from sorcerers and malevolent persons who might use personal effluvia for magical purposes.

The modern civilized world has converted the bathroom and the toilet into luxurious shrines and gleaming monuments to hygiene in enamel, marble and chrome. Jonathan Swift commented on the conspicuous elegance that people were already beginning to consider essential for such a lowly activity:

Ye great ones, why will ye disdain
To pay your tribute on the plain?
Why will you place in lazy pride
When from the homeliest earthenware?
Are sent up offerings more sincere
Than where the haughty Duchess locks
Her silver vase in a box.

Certainly the place where White Australians indulge their anal and oral fixations is opulently fitted out: not only duchesses but ordinary mortals build bathrooms of marble and mirrors and gold and silver while the main house is made of bits of timber. More a religious centre than a place simply to clean the body and deposit excrement, the bathroom has become a magical place where we indulge in secret body rituals. We clean ourselves, take our magical medicines and dispose of our magical body waste. In the marble hall we feel free to spit and gargle and pee, look at our bottoms in the mirror, touch our genitals and gaze at our latest production in the shining porcelain toilet bowl.

White Australians are in good company. Fascinated by body secretions, the Romans even had a goddess dedicated to the lowly culture of the latrine – Cloacina. The Spanish author Torquemada, quoted in Captain Bourke's book, *Scatological Rites of all Nations* devoted to the subject of body elimination, wrote that the Romans used to:

> adore . . . stinking and filthy privies and water-closets; and, what is viler and yet more abominable, what is an occasion for our tears and not to be borne with or so much as mentioned by name, they adored the noise and wind of the stomach when it expels from itself any cold or flatulence; and other things, of the same kind . . . which it would be a shame to name or describe.

White Australians would have understood the Romans! All aspects of defecation, urinating, belching and farting are material for White Australian male humour.

White Australians feel that the bathroom is not only a brilliant shrine but also a place where they can find peace and quiet, to find themselves and be themselves, to sing, to read – and even to write. To write? Yes, repressive toilet-training in western culture has given rise to a highly specialized art form, latrinalia, or writing on lavatory walls, an art form found in western culture since Roman times but not, as far as I know, in other cultures. In Australia and America nowadays so great is the desire to write on toilet walls that blackboards and chalk are often provided; the interesting fact is that the authors of this folk literature probably never write anything else.

Latrinalia, a term invented by the folklorist Alan Dundes, consists of poetry, solicitations, requests, advertisements, sad laments, jokes – the usual stereotyped symbols of White Australian and other western peoples' fixations, and good grist for an anthropologist's mill. Detailed studies of graffiti and latrinalia in western countries reveal more about their writers than any study of middle-class religious habits or family statistics. The various standard homosexual 'visiting cards' and 'invitations', for example, immediately indicate to an observer a repressed attitude to homosexuality and, paradoxically, its wide extent in the Australian suburbs.

Psychologists have suggested that writing on lavatory walls indicates an infantile desire of men – and to a much lesser extent women – to leave their mark. Young children have a natural impulse to smear their shit about, an impulse that is sublimated as they become adult. They make mud pies or model in plasticine, build sandcastles or grow up to be sculptors. In public lavatories the child-like instincts come out of hiding and men place symbolic shit – dirty words – on the walls.

Examples of latrinalia are often very funny. Some classic examples have been found throughout the Anglo-Saxon world from Tasmania to Newfoundland. One hand, for example, writes, 'I'm nine inches long and three inches round and up for sale.' Another writes in reply, 'That's fine. How big's your cock?' Many of them deal with the defecating and urinating theme, treating in particular the idea of pollution: 'No need to stand on the toilet seat,/The crabs here jump fifteen feet' refers to 'kangarooing the seat', an Australian habit in public toilets to avoid dangerous buttock-contact with the toilet; 'It does no good to line the seat,/The crabs here jump fifteen feet' refers to another common Australian-American practice of putting sheets of toilet paper on the seat to avoid contact with buttocks-crabs-shit-human filth.

Latrinalia: humour, creative impulse, or example of ambivalent attitudes to body functions? It certainly seems to reveal some odd White Australian male attitudes. Toilet behaviour, as well as toilet literature, provides interesting ethnographical material. Australian men are notorious for the long time they spend in the toilet; 'I'm reading' is the usual excuse for extending the pleasurable business of shitting. Psychologists have suggested that reading or writing while defecating is a positive action aimed at balancing the loss incurred in defecating. And why men more than women? Because men cannot give birth; they are obliged to use their anuses to provide birth substitutes – shit, like babies, comes out of a hole between the legs. Shitting thus becomes a masculine creative effort. In many ways it is similar to the Black Australian custom of the couvade.

Time, space and property

Finally, I should like to relate infantile anal obsessions among White Australians to White Australian attitudes towards time and space, property and money, and to compare these attitudes with those of Black Australians.

Our attitudes to time and money are influenced by the attitudes to defecation that we learn in early childhood. We 'pass time', we 'piddle the time away'. And like money, time is 'spent' and 'hoarded'. These phrases indicate our obsession with time and money – an obsession that parallels our obsession with faeces and urine. We impose on our bodies and on nature unnatural units of time: we divide the day, the week, the month, the year into precise units; we eat or sleep only at certain hours and 'go to the toilet' at the same time every morning.

Black Australians are, of course, conscious of time as such, but do not rigidly pattern time into morning and afternoon, working-hours, meal-times, play-time. If there is a dance or a ritual, people might take an entire day to drift in. Food is caught and eaten where it is found, at any time of the day. No one would shout 'Don't be late!', 'It's dinner *time*!', 'Don't eat between meals!' Black Australians, much more relaxed about time, toilet-training, money and property, think that the urgency felt by the Whites is rather ridiculous. White Australians must do things within a fixed time period, or before a certain deadline; they are always rushing through the day from one milestone to the next, hoping to accomplish 'something' before the end of the next artificially determined time period. But if they do, there is no time to enjoy it.

White Australians, along with other westerners, have created an artificial order of time as they have imposed an artificial order on their bodies and their bodies' functions. Black Australians celebrate natural time – the periodicity of the body, the periodicity of the female monthly cycle, the periodicity of the year and its seasons. For westerners, time goes on and on into the dreadful future, and we equip ourselves with clocks, radios, bells and observatories to keep track of the passage of time. For Black Australians, there is a steady repetition of sequences – day and night and back to day, childhood to old age and back to childhood. White Australians are future-oriented, and measure themselves in terms of how much future they have, how old they are. Blacks measure themselves in terms of the past, how many children and grandchildren they have. We reject our children and our grandchildren as signs of dreaded old age. We reject the past as we rush on into, we imagine, a better and brighter future.

In order to ensure this better future, we look forward to things, we put things aside for the future, we plan in advance when to buy a new car or go on a holiday. Then, in order to achieve these plans, we save money and time (holiday leave). In the rush, we accumulate nervous distress, nervous boredom, nervous constipation. Fearing the inability to cram all desired activities into the carefully delineated time slots allocated, White Australians have become obsessed with 'time flying', with 'wasting time', and now spend less time in bed, in the shower, or sitting quietly in the garden; even our fun and games are rushed. We have shavers that can be used while driving in the car; we have no time for church, and priests must give shortened services – drive-in churches and take-away hosts may be next. We have little time for our children who are weaned at three months and toilet-trained at about the same time to make them less of a nuisance. There is even a book called *How To Raise Children in Your Spare Time*.

White Australians and other western peoples have a quantitative approach to time, regulating it by the clock and numbers. Black Australians and other cultures have a qualitative approach: they cannot imagine time being wasted, saved or passed on as if it were property. Western ideas of time are determined by ideas of progress and financial pressures. The modern longing for a 'primitive' or more relaxed mode of existence, the growing number of successful farm communes, the hordes of drop-outs and hippies are all signs, not of a sentimental whimsicality, but of basic unsatisfied human needs to live according to more natural and human rhythms.

Just as westerners think of time as a long line with measured intervals, so they consider distance a divisible straight line, and space a measurable area. We constantly calculate distances and measures precisely, and become so fond of the habit that we tend to measure everything: the size of a friend's drawing-room, the height of a footballer, the number of slats in a wooden fence. We have become obsessional about regular, measured spaces, dividing, sub-dividing, subtracting and adding. We have numbers on the brain. For Black Australians the relevant thing about an area of land is not its size but how much food it produces, what it can be used for. And although they have a clear idea of linear order – tracks follow water-holes, camp sites and seasons – and have natural sequences in verse of a song or a ritual spell, things are not numbered or given abstract order. Numbers do not matter; it is unimportant if there are twenty-three or fifty-two kangaroos around Binji water-hole: the important point is that there are a lot of them. More-over Black Australians do not think of space in terms of artificial rectangular rooms with uniform boundaries filled with precisely arranged objects, as do White Australians, trained on the pottie to appreciate the 'neat' and 'regular'. Black Australians think of space extending into emptiness, with no closed-in areas.

As with time and space, Black Australians have a very dif-ferent, non-phobic attitude to money and property. Their bowels are not regulated by harsh methods reflecting the vagaries of the mother–child relationship but because a per-son, taught not to shame himself and others by performing these functions, goes to the outskirts of the camp. As a result a Black Australian has a sane attitude to defecation and he has the same relaxed attitude to property and money, with an emphasis on free release and exchange, rather than rigid retention. The Blacks' attitudes shock White Australians brought up on severe toilet-training methods and the prot-estant capitalist ethic. White Australians are very conscious of material wealth, and hoard property and money as signs of that wealth. We count our money, divide our money, put aside money, hide our money. We make sure that others are aware of our new elegant clothes or new bigger car, or the second or third television in the house. Among Black Australians there is little accumulation, little constipation of property and money and as a result almost no economic inequality. Every social transaction involving goods is influenced by the universal principle of sharing. In any case what would be the use of storing food and hoarding property when they would only hinder the movements of the nomadic hunter and gatherer? Therefore the Black Australian lets go of his property, as he lets go of his shit: out of natural convenience.

**Part Three
Passage to Adolescence**

Chapter Five
Boys and Girls

The infant Black Australian ceases to be a mother-clinging, female-dependent creature at a time marked by the important passage rites of weaning and toilet-training. Little boys and girls begin to walk and talk properly at about the same time as they leave the comfort of the mother's breast and begin to keep themselves clean. At an early age the boy goes off with the men on hunting trips and sleeps with his age-mates. A girl stays with her mother, accompanying the women on collecting expeditions, learning the ways of women. Gradually children become independent of their parents, although the mutual dependence of the Black family is a permanent feature of their life. No Black child ever becomes his own master as he is tied to his parents by legal and spiritual bonds even in middle-age. A White child is legally independent at eighteen; even when a Black Australian's parents are dead he still owes them respect and ritual attention, and failure to show this respect results in sanctions. White Australians honour their parents at least with token gestures at anniversaries and funerals.

Black boys gradually leave the domestic sphere, girls remain in it. During infancy the children speak their mother's language, which may be different from the father's since wives can be taken from distant, even enemy, tribes. But by the time a boy reaches puberty, he should be using his father's language as a sign of his incorporation into the world of men. Girls marry and go to live with their husbands at an early age; they pass on their mother's language to their children.

On the whole girls become women naturally: they are seen as part of Nature. Boys become men unnaturally: they are seen as belonging to Culture. Society delays manhood for youths by keeping them children until they undergo initiation rites or are sent off to war. Girls are not 'made' into women through ritual; they become women by the straightforward process of physical maturation.

Nevertheless for both boys and girls the gradual process of growing up is punctuated by the commas, semi-colons and full-stops of ritual. Little ceremonies and family feasts celebrate individual achievement. A gentle mutilation – the cutting of a lock of hair – may mark a boy's first speared goanna. When a girl catches her first fish or finds a large yam the family makes a ceremonial show of congratulation by making of a feast of these first fruits. Different stages of the period between infancy and puberty, prior to the great initiation rites and marriage, are marked by community rites and body mutilation.

Growing up is both a natural and an unnatural process. The deformation or decoration of the body plays an important part in marking new social statuses: teeth, skin, hair and body extremities are excised, patterned or altered, either to differentiate sharply the sexes or to mark particular moments in the Black Australian's physiological and cultural passage through life. The gravity of these passage rites of childhood reflect the gravity of growing up. At birth and for a period afterwards the child is considered profane, inhuman. Through ritual passages the child becomes less profane, more human: the nose is pierced, teeth are excised, the genitals mutilated.

Since women belong to nature rather than culture, they become mature with less ritual fuss: at puberty they enter the reproductive cycle, marry and begin to have children. Boys do not grow naturally into manhood. Their elders insist that they learn ritual knowledge and become scarified with the physical marks of maturity before being allowed access to adult sexuality and paternity. For boys maturity is a social fact.

All males – Black Australians, White Australians and non-human primates included – become physically mature long before they are 'made into men' and become socially adult. The juvenile period for boys ends with the eruption of a full set of permanent teeth and the onset of sexual maturity although they need not coincide exactly. However among all primates – human and non-human – sexual maturity does not mean that males are given access to females or that they are allowed to form permanent sexual unions. On the contrary, male primates become adult not when they attain the size, the strength and the secondary characteristics of physical and sexual maturity, but when their elders give them a recognized position in the social organization of the community or troop. Therefore, the ritual surrounding male maturation is much more drawn out than for females and involves a greater amount of ceremonial ritual brouhaha and physical mutilation. Boys are made into men in Black Australia by dramatic, traumatic, stigmatic initiation rites. Once upon a time, when men became men, White Australians were ripped from their mummies by the state and forced to go through the all-male agony of military service. Today initiation rites admitting growing boys into the world of grown men are individual affairs if they exist at all.

For Black Australian boys and girls socialization goes on between the punctuation marks of ceremonies. Young children learn informally through play, and imitation of older children and adults. Children are conditioned from early infancy to participate responsibly in the community, and the tasks expected of them are meaningful in both the children's and the grown-ups' worlds, although always adapted to the individual's capacity. Black children help collect food and clean animals so they are ready to be cooked. They also share in those magical activities that are not the exclusive preserve of initiated men. Their world is not alienated from that of the adults, although there is a special world of children. Songs about animals and birds, insects and fish, edible and inedible plants are taught to small children by the older ones, in the same way as White Australians learn child-lore in the playground.

The contrast between the socialization of Black and White children is very marked. White children live in a complex and disjointed world: an area is marked out 'for children' and they are expected to remain there until called by their elders or the state. White Australian children are not expected to make any positive contribution to the adult world. They do not accompany their parents to work for example; in industrial society child labour has been declared illegal and somehow has been deemed as immoral as slave labour. All the activities at the formal schools for White children have little obvious connection with everyday economic and social life. White children do not learn to grow carrots or stick pigs, make bolts or service a combustion engine. They are expected to be enthusiastic about theoretical mathematics and French, though they are thousands of miles from France and few will become Professors of Pure Maths. And they learn to swim and run and jump, not in rivers and paddocks, but in artificial basins and fenced-in sports fields.

What are the incentives and what are the rewards? The ceremonial feast of congratulation when a Black child spears his first kangaroo is far removed from our competitive examination system. In White society children are spurred on to be successful: successful at school, successful at sports, successful in the social ring. And being successful means winning, 'coming first', coming 'top'. We have to be champions or geniuses to win a grudging word of congratulation from our parents or teachers who want children to be Einsteins or Wimbledon champions. I went in for the Einstein race and my brother chose Wimbledon and we are still on the hopeless march, struggling to come to terms with these impossible goals. We fought for academic medals and sporting trophies at the expense of relaxed and expressive personalities. From personal experience I am convinced that the constant competition in school and sports results in emotional backwardness and moral insensibility among us White Australians. Black Australians manage to avoid these difficulties.

Sex roles

Learning sex roles and learning sex is an important part of growing up. Although Black boys and girls, before their marriage or initiation, are grouped together as 'women', they begin to learn their separate roles when they begin to untie the close physical bonds with their mothers. As soon as they can walk, girls are given digging sticks, the female symbol *par excellence*, and sent off to get women's food and do women's work: digging up edible roots or the larvae of ants, collecting small game. The boys are given spears and begin to hunt and fight mock battles. Even in their play rituals, children imitate male and female adult roles: girls cluster together and imitate female mourners wailing and tearing at their bodies around a corpse, while boys perform men's activities – preparing the body for burial, imitating the dirges. The girls dance, the boys sing and the small babies, not yet 'boys' or 'girls', clap in appreciation.

Among White Australians there is a half-hearted attempt to separate little boys from little girls; they are sometimes dressed in blue or pink as the case may be – little-boy and little-girl clothes – but many parents no longer insist on strict sexual role segregation and there are certainly no ceremonies or rituals to make boys boys or girls girls. Sex role behaviour is taught in less institutionalized ways, particularly through peer group pressure like name-calling ('cissy' or 'butch'). In some cases, given the unisex hair-dos and clothing, it appears that many adolescent Whites make little sexual differentiation at all. This new phenomenon – which begins in childhood with boys playing with dolls and girls with toy tractors – is called 'gender softening' by sociologists. White Australians and westerners on the whole are decreasing the emphasis on different roles, and sexual lines are becoming crossed and sometimes confused. The ritual use of the great Dr Spock by the middle classes, the involvement of fathers in domestic activities and mothers working all contribute to the erosion of some of the rigid male-female gender differences.

Sexual behaviour is not instinctual, but like most human activities, it has to be taught and learned. The very experience of sexual excitement which White Australians fondly imagine springs from hidden internal sources is in fact learned behaviour. How do we learn about it?

Most people do it by the traditional learning methods of play and imitation. Even among non-human primates it has been found that sex, like aggression and maternal feelings, is not an instinctual activity but is acquired. Macaque rhesus monkeys learn about sex at an early age, even before they are capable of the physical act; infants and juveniles copy their elders, mounting each other and giving comic pelvic thrusts. Zoologists have discovered that if monkeys do not learn their proper sexual roles in childhood or at least before they become sexually mature, they never develop completely normal patterns; raised in isolation monkeys simply can't do it properly. In wild primate groups, they grow up in a social setting where adult copulatory behaviour can be observed. Is there a lesson for us here? Are we also in danger of forgetting the art of sex because we have no one to imitate, having only porno films and sex shop material as resources.

Black Australians learn about sex as casually as they learn to hunt and gather food. As in African communities that I have observed, small boys and girls imitate the act of love long before they are competent to perform it properly or before they are even sexually aroused. Except in the presence of tabooed relatives, the physical relations between men and women are talked about cheerfully and without embarrassment, not ignored or discussed in veiled language as among White Australians. In this way children soon become familiar with the facts of sex and the anatomy of the opposite sex. Since girls are usually more mature than boys they may instigate the sex games and teach the boys the techniques. Small children play at sex in groups; when they grow older they do it in private without any sense of guilt or shame induced by disapproving adult attitudes. Black Australian parents positively try to prevent any feelings of guilt and shame about sexuality; childish masturbation finds an amused, not a shocked, audience and adults soothe fretful children by gently stroking their sex organs.

My personal experience provides a strange contrast. The basic premise of parents and schoolteachers in Tasmania was that sex was dirty, rather funny or merely taboo; whatever it was, sexuality was to be guessed by children rather than learned. Sex education was minimal in order to lessen the need for physical expression; there was the common, erroneous idea that sex education put ideas rather than facts into little heads. And while my parents and teachers vaguely hoped I should remain innocent, I and my friends fumbled around in the dark, waiting for something to happen – which it never did. We were like the isolated rhesus macaque monkeys lost in the gloomy world of youthful sexuality with no one to watch or imitate. Even now, knowing that children often learn about sex by watching their own parents, the idea of my own parents making love is quite ungraspable.

We looked for models in novels and romantic films. We stalked courting lovers along the beach. We watched cows and dogs and fowls. I read in child management manuals that masturbating boys should be directed to toys. The first naked woman I saw was a seventy-year-old great-aunt having a bath; I watched her with my cousin through a sky-light and almost fell through it with shock. Finally when I was old enough to be a father of a child of seven, I found out what I wanted and went twelve thousand miles away to get it.

The great pall of prudery was lifted in the 'sexy sixties'. In the 1940s, Tasmania and, to a lesser extent, the rest of Australia was in the grip of a puritanical obsession known as wowserism. It was as if the taboos of medieval christianity had been swept up and dumped on the green little 'Apple Island'. Were there really taboos that forbade sex after eating, sex before eating, sex in the daytime, sex with the light on, sex without trousers on, sex on Sundays, during Lent, before and after going to church? Certainly most innocent pleasures were tainted with sinfulness and banned. Drinking sherry, instead of being a social activity, became a sin; gambling a crime. A drop of alcohol never entered our weatherboard sanctum of sexual and moral purity. On Sundays we dressed in shiny serge and went to Sunday school and church; we were forbidden to run down the hill and play football, go to the shop to buy an ice cream, go to the cinema. What a different world in Africa and Italy, where children of five are allowed wine with their water, soccer on Sundays and fun and games when they want. Even Tasmania has changed of course; if you ask a child if he goes to Sunday school, he may say yes, but he may mean he accompanies his parents to an illicit drinking den since the hotels are still shut on Sunday mornings.

Black Australians of all ages have a healthy partiality for sex, and obscenity as well. Their religious myths are full of bizarre sexual imagery. When White Australians learn of the erotic myths and poetry of Black Australians or read about the sexuality of their religious rites, they are shocked; they are usually christians who have not read the Song of Solomon, the story of Saint Theresa or the details of the erotic elements in Indian, Greek and Roman rituals. White Australians express their basic need for obscenity in bar-room dirty jokes and in the infantile pornography of men-only magazines.

Sex in Black Australia is liberated. Boys and girls are 'de-virginized' without much fuss or individual preoccupation, usually at an early age with a favoured companion. In White Australia, even in the 1970s, young people still experience their first orgasm in a bewildering number of decidedly exotic ways: solitary masturbation, tumbling with a pet, horseplay with members of one's own sex, heavy petting in a motor car, dry fucking, finger fucking – almost anything but straightforward civilized copulation. Adolescent sex and a lot of adult sex is a miserable, half-hearted activity plagued by ignorance, guilt and fears of impotence, pregnancy or disease.

While sex for Black Australians may be fun and guiltless, it is not the constant orgy of unrestricted promiscuity that many White Australians fondly imagine. Once boys have been initiated, and girls married, they learn to take sex more seriously. But even before then, when young people have affairs, although there may be no disapproval, parents and kin ensure that the lovers are properly matched according to the criteria for marriage based on membership of totemic moieties. Children are taught the laws of adultery and incest, and which partners they may have sex with, which they may not; they learn that sex is not merely a biological activity but a cultural one which has to be channelled in certain directions and sometimes even sublimated. In general, the sexual taboos follow the marriage rules: a man cannot marry or have intercourse with the daughter of any kinsman he calls 'father' or with any kinswoman he calls 'mother' – they are his sisters, however distant the relationship. Cross-cousins, however, both near and distant, may be courted since they are expected to marry: cross-cousins are the children of married siblings of the opposite sex. These sex taboos and marriage prescriptions have to be learned and although they may be often broken – like all taboos – they govern much of the social behaviour of the community. The most tabooed relative for men is the 'mother-in-law' category; mothers-in-law may not be spoken to, eaten with, or even looked at.

Nineteenth-century White Australians threw up their over-dressed arms in horror at the sexual practices of Black Australians, practices which would hardly raise an eyebrow in Melbourne suburbs today. And they wrote with bemused paternalism of their sexual taboos. However Black Australians were just as bemused. They watched the White missionaries – men who preached morals and good living and the wearing of clothes – sharing a house with their mother, their grown-up sisters and their mother-in-law, sharing the same food, the same bathroom in the greatest intimacy. They saw that White men set at nought every taboo the Blacks held holy. From the Blacks' point of view the missionaries were living in a kind of promiscuous group marriage; they were sex maniacs in black suits who showed the greatest disrespect for their mother-in-law by sitting opposite her at table and sharing food with her.

The Black Australians also watched White Australians come and take their land, and their sisters and their daughters as concubines. This was all right. But when White Australians took tabooed women, they breached Black law and religion, and this 'crime' was punishable by death. It was as if a man had set up house in a comfortable Sydney suburb with his eight-year-old granddaughter as his mistress.

Girls into women

The lives of Black women, even more so than their White sisters, are determined by their bodies and their physiological processes. At menarche – first menstruation – they are automatically declared socially and physically mature with a certain amount of ceremony, and until the menopause, they are tied to their menstrual periodicity and to their performance as mothers. Black girls have no formal initiation at puberty but are simply induced into the private, domestic world of married women with children, while their brothers are initiated into the public sphere of adult men which excludes women and children.

Of course White women are also victims of their bodies and of men's attitudes to their bodies; the definiteness of the physiological changes seems to give them some kind of advantage and they succeed in arriving at adulthood without the floating sense of hopelessness that most boys experience. Although this judgement is probably subjective, Australian girls seem to grow up and mature earlier and have steadier characters and stronger personalities than their brothers. Girls are considered reasonable creatures; boys are unreasonable and controlled with difficulty through rewards, deprivation and direct punishment. In Black Australia they go through aggressive and violent initiation ceremonies.

Certain Black girls grow up more quickly than boys, come to maturity early, indulge in sex-play with lovers, and have what appears to be a programmed adolescent sterility that protects them from having babies when they are very young. They are married and go to their husbands at nine or ten, have a child at fifteen or sixteen and assume full adult female status. As a being of Nature, rather than Culture, a girl's physical development is noted and rewarded. A girl whose breasts begin to develop is given a special name; and when they begin to hang slightly pendant, the characteristic form of an adult woman, she is given another. Special names and ceremonies clearly indicate the girl's development in procreative ability, in her natural capacity to have children. The physical signs of maturity are much more dramatic than they are for a boy: a girl's pelvis enlarges and her limbs round out with fat; her breasts enlarge as a result of the development of gland tissue and her hair becomes more luxuriant. Throughout the world the greater emphasis on rites for boys and young men may be because male physical development is less marked. There is no exact moment parallel to menstruation, for example, when a boy can say, 'Look! I'm a man'; the passage is accomplished artificially by circumcision and other kinds of transfiguration of a cultural kind.

In western societies where fertility and motherhood are no longer the great desiderata for women, the startling natural facts of physical development among girls and women are concealed. In White Australia a woman's menarche is ignored by the community; pregnancies are rarely celebrated or flaunted in public; matrescence is no longer the great public ceremonial event it used to be. Her breasts, instead of hanging down as a sign of a long and fruitful life are carefully packaged to look like those of a young, infertile girl. Statuses which are sources of satisfaction for 99 per cent of the women of the world – motherhood followed by grandmotherhood – fill her with terror and she dyes her hair, often dresses like a much younger woman and insists that her grandchildren call her by her first name instead of by a title indicating her position of respected elder. Her menopause, when she ceases to be procreative, is supposed to be completely ignored by everyone but her closest associates.

White Australian women artificially delay growing up and growing old; in great contrast, Black Australian girls marry at ten and flaunt their elderly maternity at twenty. White Australian law makes it illegal for a mature woman of fifteen to make love. A striking feature of Australian towns are the beautiful mature women walking around in school uniforms, their breasts concealed in pleated tunics and their hair in infantile plaits. Although girls are told that they wear uniforms to promote pride in their school, the uniform in fact symbolizes the remarkable situation whereby grown women are kept at school when they might be copulating and reproducing. Boys too are restrained from 'adult' activities, but this case is not so exceptional in ethnography: in some societies, men of thirty are still viewed as children if they have not yet married and had children of their own. I myself wore childish boots, childish long socks and short trousers when I left school at seventeen, and even today men with moustaches and great calf muscles walk around in quaint boy-scout uniforms and little-boy school-caps. Physically adults, these White Australians are socially little boys and little girls. Yet they are the cultural inheritors of Helen of Troy who was married at ten and had wars fought for her at thirteen.

If girls are to be kept down sexually, the physical signs of their sexual maturity – the menarche and menstruation – must be hidden. Where girls are more liberated sexually – that is, in most other parts of the world – menstruation, particularly first menstruation, is an occasion which is always noted, whether it is seen as a blessing or a dreadful threat or both. Among Black Australians, the menarche is publicly celebrated and is a matter for congratulation; the girl, adorned with ritual body decoration and a ceremonial nairdo, is grandly presented to her kin and to her husband as an adult woman. A White Australian girl is propelled into adulthood on high heels – symbol of her subjection to men – and with a splash of red – an unconscious symbol of menstruation? – on her lips. A White girl is not congratulated, publicly or privately, when she reaches the menarche; the only clues her brothers may have are her coy remarks such as 'I can't come swimming today'

A Black Australian girl celebrates the menarche individually. Prior to the ceremony she retires to a secluded part of the camp or bush with her mother or an older female relative who teaches her what she must do and tells her that she is in a sacred, dangerous state. She learns that she must not go near water-holes while she is menstruating and she must not touch a man, for he would go grey at once. She learns that she must not dig yams or cook food or even touch it with her hands; nor should she make a fire, touch water or even look at stretches of water. My sisters were given similar admonishments: they were told not to swim or wash their hair, arrange fresh flowers or chop up fresh meat. The Black Australian girl is told how to stop the flow squatting over a hollow with a fire of green twigs; then she is covered from the waist down in sand and surrounded by a fence; she is secluded and allowed to speak only to her female companions. The older women use this occasion to impress upon the girl the need to follow the group's moral and religious code particularly as far as sexual conduct is concerned. From now on promiscuous sex-play ends, in theory, and the girl becomes a respectable married woman; nobody, of course, expects her to give up lovers and adulterous liaisons.

After this period of seclusion the girl is bathed and she makes a public entry into the main camp; the other women accompany her and sing ceremonial songs. She is richly decorated and after the procession she is acclaimed as a woman and an adult. On Melville Island the girl is painted in red and yellow by the father who also dresses her hair and builds it up into a mop by twisting it in curled strands of human hair on top of a bamboo chaplet; on the top of this is fixed an ornament of flattened dogs' tails set in beeswax. Although a woman is not permitted to acquire all the sacred knowledge of the group, as an adult her ritual education continues after this ceremony of the menarche, and she gradually takes part in women's ceremonies and fulfils a subsidiary role in men's ritual performances.

Black Australians have an ambivalent attitude to menstruation and menstrual blood, considering it both a blessing and a curse, not just a 'curse' as it is to White Australians.* Menstrual blood pollutes but also has benevolent powers; it brings life and saves life. Menstrual blood, for example, is given to a man who is too ill to eat. When Black women are secluded at menstruation this seclusion indicates the awe rather than the horror with which men view them. Menstruation is, in a sense, celebrated as a sign of femininity and not only as a sign of an inferior polluting sex.

This ambivalent attitude to menstruation is found among many peoples, although its nature as a curse has always had the bigger press. Sex with menstruating women is almost universally avoided and it has even been suggested in the name of scientific medicine that coitus with a menstruating

---

*Italian women had a pleasant belief about menstruation: it was said that at her monthly period each woman rose a step in the social hierarchy – peasant women became ladies (*signore*); ladies became noble women (*nobile donne*); noble women became queens and queens became madonnas.

woman may be dangerous to the male: it is said that penile contact with the discharge may lead to urethritis, an inflammation of part of the urinary tract. Moreover, the menstrual fluid, which consists of blood, tiny broken down particles of the uterine lining and a certain amount of mucus, also contains bacteria and may be infectious to open wounds. This scientific hypothesis is part of the civilized 'hygiene theory' of sexual taboos and social behaviour. Like shit, menstrual blood is considered dirty, dangerous, polluting, because it is needed as a symbol of the 'dirty, dangerous, polluting' nature of women. Pliny wrote that contact with menstrual blood turned new wine sour, crop plants touched by it became barren, grafts died, seed in gardens dried up, the fruit of trees fell off. And dogs, if they tasted it, became mad and their bites were infected with poison.

Marriage for Black Australians may occur before or after the menarche. Formal betrothal occurs when the girl is a few months or a year old. Her future husband brings her family cooked food, kangaroo and emu meat, red ochre, skeins of hairstring, boomerangs and spears; the child is formally presented and her mother prepares a gift of food for her son-in-law. For seven or eight years the husband may not see much of his wife although he continues to send presents, particularly to his mother-in-law. When the girl is about nine she begins to visit her husband, gradually spending longer periods until she finally remains with him, usually after the menarche.

Before she begins to co-habit with her husband, however, she may herself already be a mother-in-law, a status which because of certain Black Australian marriage customs, she can acquire at any age after five. In ceremonial finery the small girl is presented to her son-in-law, a man between twenty and thirty, by her father who places an elaborately carved spear between her legs; then he presents it to his daughter's son-in-law who calls the spear his wife. This ritual expresses the promise of the girl to give her first daughter in marriage to this man. For the girl, this is an exciting passage rite and she takes on the role of putative mother-in-law happily enough since her son-in-law now accepts some responsibility for her, providing her with special food and ornaments and other welcome services throughout her life.

Menarche, breasts, marriage, mother-in-lawdom are all signs of a girl's maturation. Accompanying these changes are other ceremonies, many of which involve physical mutilation. She has her nose pierced and a quill introduced into the wound; she is given a special name. She has one – or both – of her upper incisor teeth removed as a further sign of maturity. There is no evidence that Black Australians have ever subjected their women to true female circumcision; however, removal of parts of White Australian female genitalia and reproductive system, usually at the time of the menopause, is not uncommon.

A form of mutilation of the vagina is practised by both Black and White Australians. White Australian women are mutilated during labour by the unnatural rite of episiotomy. Some Black women undergo a similar physical operation before they marry. In north-western Queensland introcision of the vagina is performed – the posterior vaginal margin, known as the fourchette, is torn and the hymen artificially ruptured. This ceremonial 'opening of the vagina' is considered a precondition of marital sex – not sex – as well as of pregnancy and is an important ritual occasion. The men who do it – like the surgeons in the White hospitals – say they do it to make sex and child-bearing easier for the women; just as some White women claim that episiotomy makes childbirth easier for the obstetrician, Black women say that men do the introcision to make intercourse easier for them. Usually the operation is done with a stick in the shape of a penis. Among the Aranda, two or three men, on behalf of the husband, enlarge the vaginal orifice by pushing down the first three fingers round which they have wound possum string. And in other groups, it is the husband himself who 'deflowers' the girl with his finger.

For Black Australian girls, maturity, as we have seen, is primarily a physical fact. They menstruate and become women, marry and begin to reproduce. Women are tied to their physical, natural functions and for them – at least in Black and White Australia – there are no initiation rites or secret lodges at adolescence. Women have been condemned to their roles as 'fertile bodies' and it is only recently that White women have ceased to accept a definition of themselves as mothers, sexual objects and housewives. A generation ago White women, like their Black sisters, were also confined to biological and sexual roles; as children they played with dolls and became 'little mothers' at six. They accepted as natural their feminine personalities, their irrationality and their enforced association with the physical and the natural – birth, toilet-training, food, dirt. Even modern family counsellors, led by Dr Spock, have glorified feminine domesticity thereby imprisoning women in the home with their babies. Westerners are even given money by governments to stay at home and be fertile. They make jams and knit bootees and join women's clubs to compare their skill at cake-making and breast-feeding. The woman's role in White Australia is impressed on the bride-to-be by 'showers' – ritual occasions when her female friends and relatives help her to furnish her prison-temple (her home) with gleaming pots and pans, tea-sets and crystal fruit bowls. Later her commitment to her marriage, her family and her home is ceremonially renewed when the birth of a baby stimulates a new round of gifts and cards and congratulations.

White women are expected to keep the home fires burning, and so are Black. However Black women are in no way restricted to domestic roles and are not kept at home. They are fully independent workers who provide more than half the family livelihood. Black women are not dependent on their husbands for their subsistence. Although they may not spear kangaroos or catch large fish, they collect all the vegetable food and small game animals like bandicoots, possums and goannas.

Basically, though, women are confined to natural, female functions and trained for the natural, the profane world. Men inhabit a different world, a world of religion, initiation rites and war, and they are trained for the cultural, sacred world. Black Australian youths are initiated into religious secrets by men; White Australian men are the priests, the freemasons and the soldiers. In Black Australia and White

Australia, woman is the giver of life, while her husband, the superior creature, is the killer. Because killing is incompatible with the ideals of motherhood, fertile women are denied entry into secret male societies, denied an active role in war, denied a role as huntress. In Black Australia, the men are killers with spears and their wives have digging sticks; in White Australia, the men are killers with guns and their wives have pots and pans and knitting needles.

In the totemic lodges and drinking clubs, to which women are forbidden membership, Black and White men alike invent a secret world of their own and talk of sex and war. Both Black Australians (during the initiation rites) and White Australians (in their hotels, their sports clubs, their ex-soldiers associations) hide away together and permit themselves the luxury of talking big, imagining themselves superior to and independent of their women folk.

Chapter Six
Physical Symbols

The great Black Australian initiation rites, involving circumcision and subincision, mark young men's social rather than physical maturation; in the next chapter I shall look closely at the symbolism involved in this cultural event. Here I want to look at one or two more minor ceremonies which coincide with physical rather than social growth and which are marked by bodily mutilation. My express purpose is to compare 'barbaric' rites performed by Black and White Australians: ear-piercing and nose-piercing; scarification and tattooing; ritual tooth excision and finger-lopping. Although an anthropologist, I am personally perhaps poorly qualified to write about circumcision, tattooing and other ritual mutilations as my body has so far been almost untouched by ritual or cosmetic surgery. I have not been scarified or tattooed; my ears are unpierced; my body has no ceremonial or duelling scars; my extremities are all intact. To some African people, I am a rare, untouched canvas, slightly inhuman: uncircumcised, teeth unfiled (like a dog), my pinkish skin plain and unadorned (like a pig).

Most peoples however insist on converting the natural body into a cultural body by mutilation, decoration or excision. It seems there is a basic need to alter the animal body, to disfigure and to figure our skin. A young White Australian who wants to have his ears pierced will not accept screw-back earrings; it is the hole he wants. Both Black and White men and women are made into complete people through the marking of their bodies; the ceremony and the marking affect the mentality of the initiates. The unadorned, natural human body has never been considered sufficiently attractive or meaningful by any human group, including our own, to leave it in its 'natural' state; body decoration has been used everywhere to turn the bestial body into a human

body. For some White Australians, wary of permanent alter-
ations to their body, most cultural messages are sent by
clothes and hairstyles, cosmetics and suntan, although cosmetic surgery, ear-piercing and tattooing are exact counterparts to Black Australian nose-piercing, scarification and
finger-lopping. Among both peoples these mutilations occur
most frequently at crisis moments: during puberty, at the
threshold of social adulthood, marriage, sexual initiation,
childbirth, the menopause. The meaning of these mutilations
is not explained solely by the physical action of pulling out
hair, cutting the body or smartening up breasts and buttocks.
As Aristotle said of the Greek mysteries, 'The initiated do
not learn anything so much as feel certain emotions and are
put in a certain frame of mind.' The frame of mind is sometimes achieved by mutilation. The removal of a tooth during
puberty is the external mark; the pain and the ritual help
mark a stage of physical and social growth. At initiation a
Black Australian boy leaves the women's camp a naked child
and comes back a circumcised adult.

Teeth

The body is not only frequently used to demonstrate special
states and statuses, it is also moulded by massage and even
surgery to resemble the ideal shape appreciated by a certain
society. Black Australian midwives attempt to flatten the
baby's nose; they also mould the penis and clitoris to socially-
accepted forms. White Australians mould the head of a new-
born baby into what is considered the ideal Caucasian shape;
the foreskin of the penis may be removed, for cultural, not
hygienic reasons.

The first Black Australian ceremony involving bodily
mutilation is usually the piercing of the nose septum, a rite
that apparently has little more symbolic significance than
ear-piercing for little European and African girls. The nose,
oddly enough, is the most common object for cosmetic surgery among White Australians; a painful operation is carried
out on a part of the body Freudians have always associated
with the genitals. This operation is supposed to improve an
individual's general and sexual attractiveness.

As I have already pointed out girls arrive at sexual maturity suddenly, at the menarche; boys mature more gradually. Apart from the slow signs of manhood associated with the growth of pubic hair, facial hair and a deepening of the voice, the acquisition of a full set of permanent teeth is the only other clear physical mark of adulthood. As a sign of social maturity, not only is their sex mutilated – in circumcision and vagina stretching – but Black children of both sexes have one or two of the permanent canine or incisor teeth removed in a ceremony performed by kinsmen.

The operation is straightforward and the ritual minimal. The child is taken to a special spot by his cross-cousin, usually one of 'mother's brother's sons'; he lies on his back on the ground, held down tightly by other relatives. The operator-dentist carefully strips back the gum from around the tooth with a sharp, pointed stick. The stick is pressed against the tooth and hit with a stone until the tooth is loose enough to be removed with the fingers; it is then held up in triumph for everyone to see.

Barbaric, primitive, irrational behaviour? Feeling the typical White Australian reaction of nervous disgust at the thought of the operation, the torn flesh, pain and blood, particularly in association with the sacred Australian orifice, the mouth, I tried to persuade myself to be objective and to look at our own savage attacks on our bodies, our own barbaric, primitive and irrational operations. What is our reaction to cosmetic surgery on the nose if it is described in this cold-blooded, ethnographic way? Thinking about tooth extraction, I recalled my own childhood. I was thirteen and struggling like a tadpole out of water into adulthood; I was having an awful time and so were my parents. My beautiful set of white teeth seemed to be my only asset. One day after a family conference, my father took me to the local dentist who extracted an incisor tooth: the same incisor tooth that a Black Australian's 'mother's brother's son' extracts from his cross-cousin's mouth. Once again the famous White Australian 'hygiene theory' was given as an excuse: my father told the dentist, an elderly, old-fashioned small-town tooth-puller, that my mouth was getting too full for my beautiful white teeth; the dentist agreed that room should be made for the great white molars and canines. So terrified was I of the grotesque image of my mouth being filled with monstrous stalactites and stalagmites that I made no gallant stand against going under gas for the ritual mutilation. I went through a few moments or an eternity of anaesthetized phantasmagoria – just as the Black Australian child must experience a moment of unanaesthetized phantasmagoria – with the faces of my father and his stooge looming down at me. I came to without a healthy front tooth. My father was content; I went home sobered, less wild with puberty. I have been left with a crooked but half-empty mouth as a sign of a private adolescent rite of passage.

I was struck by this coincidence and mentioned Black Australian tooth excision to a friend of mine who came up with the usual, stock, unthinking answer: 'Poor things, they use their bodies like a painter uses a canvas, or a sculptor a lump of clay. They lop off fingers, knock out teeth, score their arms and legs with burning sticks and stone knives, cut up their penises.' I thought of members of my family who had had their noses straightened, foreskin removed, ears pierced, ovaries out, arms tattooed, breasts smartened up. I told him that when I was thirteen my father took me to the dentist who removed one of my front teeth. 'Oh, yes,' he said. 'We White Australians have small jaws and large teeth.' It turned out that he had just taken his thirteen year old son to a dentist in Tasmania to have his two upper and two lower canines removed, for 'hygienic reasons'.

Quite obviously both Black and White Australians remove healthy teeth for symbolic reasons. My mother had all her teeth taken out on the doctor's advice when she had incessant migraines during the menopause; same dentist, same 'hygiene theory'. Healthy teeth are taken out by Whites and the reasons stated are medical; healthy teeth are taken out by Black Australians and the reasons, if any, are symbolic and magical. An anthropologist must try to be objective and compare the two experiences as carefully as possible. The teeth of menopausal women are removed to prevent headaches. The teeth of White children at puberty are removed on the flimsiest of excuses, by a dentist on behalf of the parents, usually the father, in an impressive and traumatic ceremony. Among Black Australians, the operation is performed by a relative, not a sadistic local dentist. Instead of being strapped in a giant chair with metallic objects swinging at him and gas hissing, the Black boy is held in the arms of relatives. A relative fills the boy's mouth with fur-string to absorb blood and deaden the pain in the same way as swabs of cotton were forced into my mouth. When I came out of the whizzing, swirling, magical gasdream, I was given my poor tooth and I carried it around as a memento of my lost childhood for a day or two. The Black dentist holds up the tooth with a triumphant shout and throws it as far as possible in the direction of the mother's totemic field.

In 1977 I was able to talk to one or two enlightened dentists, who provided a welcome contrast to the witch-doctors of Tasmania in the 1940s. They assured me that it is not necessary to remove youngsters' front teeth on account of crowding, just as it is not necessary to remove a male child's foreskin for hygienic reasons. The belief that White jaws are getting smaller and teeth bigger is a White Australian folk belief – and a common one – connected with the doubts and fears of parents and children during puberty. The dental specialist told me that one of his most common tasks was to deal with the distorted jaws of young people whose teeth have been removed by foolish dentists on the insistence of foolish parents. He mentioned the case of a child of twelve: the boy had already had an operation to prevent his ears from sticking out too much and his mother had insisted that his buck teeth be straightened – the local dentist removed two back molars so that the brace could be put in. The child went around with a metal support for his ears and an iron brace in his mouth. All the dentists could do for the many women who had no teeth at all was give them shining new dentures.

As the dentist pointed out to me, the removal of teeth or the straightening of teeth seemed to satisfy some deep desire on the part of the parents of the pubescent child to leave a physical mark on their son or daughter, possibly as a reaction to the onset of puberty and the prospect of independence. The removal of teeth at the menopause indicated to me a need to make some mutilation of the body at another period of crisis. Circumcision of baby boys at the request of the mother is a symbolic, magical operation which satisfies the need for physical alteration of the body as an expression of the passage rite of maternity and as a symbol of maternal control of the child. Does ritual excision of the teeth of children and menopausal women achieve the same result?

Anthropologists usually maintain that physical mutilation at puberty – for example, the removal of teeth – marks the physical and social maturation of the child, the passing of the boy or girl into the rank of adults. The Black Australian rite seems to support the theory that mutilation symbolizes the removal of the neutral, androgynous child from the world of women, since the tooth is thrown in the direction of the mother's totemic field. For the anthropologist, therefore, the extraction of teeth and the cutting of the penis are arbitrary signs indicating a status change: the passage from adolescence to adulthood, and from adulthood to old age, I suppose, in the case of my mother's mutilation. The mutilated individual is removed from the common mass of humanity by a rite of separation, which is the basic idea behind the cutting, the piercing, the extraction. The transfigured person is re-incorporated into a defined group – the operation leaves ineradicable traces making the incorporation therefore permanent.

On the other hand psychologists are interested in the symbolic meaning of the mutilated parts of the body: why the nose, the ear, the penis, the mouth? As far as White Australians are concerned, the mouth is almost as important a magical – and erogenous – zone as the genitalia. Our worry over its appearance and health go far beyond a natural concern for cleanliness. Our mouth rituals in our marble bathrooms, our sprays and massages and brushing reveal a pathological horror of and fascination with the mouth. Without purity of mouth, our world would collapse: husbands would leave wives, girls would never accept the advances of boys, nobody would get a job or pass exams or even be able to get on a bus with confidence. Naturally enough, if sadistic parents want to put their mark on their children, or men on their women-folk during their fractious menopausal days, the mouth is the place to do it.

Even today I remember with a tremble the crunch of the roots of my tooth meeting the iron surgical pincers; the distorted face of my father peering down, the wild dreams, the hallucinating smell of the gas, all the blood. Recently it has been found – heaven knows how – that babies who have been circumcised sleep more heavily, as if drugged, after the operation, than uncircumcised babies. Perhaps tooth extraction calms wild children or wild middle-aged women, making them more malleable to their parents' or husbands' wishes. In the nineteenth century, obstreperous wives had their ovaries whipped out at the slightest sign of hysteria or opposition to their master-husband.

This argument, at least as far as it concerns tooth extraction, receives some support from Freudian theory – but then which argument doesn't. This theory interprets the removal of teeth as part of an initiation ritual which symbolizes castration or genital elimination, like circumcision. Accordingly, a tooth is a genital symbol, a penis that fathers remove out of jealousy of the maturing adolescent son, or that husbands remove from a sexually disturbed wife. By taking out a tooth, Black and White jealous fathers are emasculating their rival sons: instead of the initiation rite making men out of boys, it makes eunuchs out of boys. Just as there is always a Freudian theory to support every sociological argument, so is there always a Greek myth to support a Freudian theory. In an ancient Greek myth about male procreation, men sowed dragon's incisors–penises in order to produce all-male offspring! White Australians feel that the removal of the fierce, predatory incisors gives a girlier, rather than 'all-male', look to the virile mouth. I shall have a closer look at the feminizing aspects of initiation rites and associated womb envy in the next chapter.

Body marks

The human body is altered for many reasons, and one of

the major ones, of course, is for decoration – 'art for art's sake', not art for Freud's sake. As Captain Cook said of the Patagonians, 'they are content to be naked but ambitious to be fine.' Circumcision, the scoring of the body in patterns of parallel lines, sub-incision, tooth extraction are all linked to the male ideal of beauty. Mutilation is designed to make men attractive to women. Black Australians, however, are rarely 'naked'. Except as small children, they are completely naked only on special occasions; the anxious father, for example, strips when waiting the birth of his child. A young girl at puberty wears an apron belt although some people may consider the pubic hair and a simple tassel sufficient covering. A man also wears a pubic tassel after he reaches adulthood and like those White Australian women who feel naked without a hat, is rarely seen without his hair head-band. Hair, like clothing, may also indicate status. The usual style of a Black small boy's hair is a top-knot. At puberty, youths begin to pull out the hair on their foreheads to make it appear loftier; they draw back the hair and fasten it with a band smeared with red ochre. A handsome Black man has no hair on his forehead, his face, his pubes or his armpits; a handsome White Australian has hair in all these places and he does not pluck his high forehead but pulls his sparse hair forward. No hair, like a polluting mouth, has come to signify social ostracism, sexual failure and unemployment through old age and retirement.

Hair for Black and White Australians is endowed with per-sonality and is good material – like bodily excretions – for symbolic expression: it can be plucked, cut, curled, put into shapes, dyed, shaved. White Australians use it to indicate gender, youth, rebellion. Other peoples use it to mark marriage, maternity, old age. Hair on the body of Black Aus-tralians is not a sign of masculinity and it is removed; hair on the body of White Australian women is un-feminine and it is removed. Long hair, hanging down over the ears, was once thought a suitable style for nubile maidens in White Australia; now it is worn by young, and not so young, men and women alike.

The adolescents of the world's big metropoles today use

their bodies to express deprivation, political faiths, or just themselves as individuals. In London, Sydney and New York, young people are obsessed with their bodies: hair is dyed half blond, half red; tattoos for boys and girls give them a sense of identity. Body painting sets revolutionary youth apart from the middle-class suburban world. Rome youths of the left and right set themselves apart with hair-dos and hair-dyes. Even the middle-aged, middle-class suburban world has its body obsessions: skin is expanded and contracted, stretched and shrunk and peeled through surgery, dyed and bleached through ritual cosmetics; fasting and feasting changes the body's shape which is squeezed into corsets and tight trousers. Hair, face, breast, stomach, buttocks, even hands and feet are altered. Our general dissatisfaction with our natural human shape results from a mythical White Australian ideal of the lithe, golden blond body that is impossible to attain without painful exercise, dieting, operation or plain fraud. White Australians normally develop fat legs and fat ankles and fat thighs, and have thin shoulders and flaccid biceps. White men and women consciously and unconsciously spend a considerable part of every day trying to achieve an impossible ideal. They battle with a natural flabbiness and slumpiness, jogging in parks, pressing up in gyms. Hairstyles are changed, moustaches grown, beards shaved off; and the body is submitted to long periods of masochistic sun-tanning. Unfortunately, unlike the Black Australians, the Whites' physique is not adapted to the sunny Australian desert climate and they become over-baked and pink – blonds in a brown man's climate.

All this is very unnatural and even magical. Just as Black Australians 'work on' their bodies, so also do we grapple in a formless, unritualized way with our poor bodies, in a hopeless struggle towards purity and perfection. We are obsessed with our mouths and other orifices, pimples and dandruff, bad breath and body smells, too much hair or too little hair in the wrong places. All deviations from the ideal are a threat: if you are too fat or too thin, slant-eyed or black, crippled or over-toothed, you become a feared and guilty source of danger not only to yourself but to your neighbours and your friends – and to the ideal image of the blond, bronzed White Australian 'fetichized' on the advertisement hoardings.

Black Australians, unlike White Australians have formalized and ritualized their need to come to terms with their body and to figure it. Bodily mutilation for Blacks occurs at times of status changes recognized by the community. The body is scarified as a sign of initiation, ritual elderhood, mourning. While bodily mutilation of White Australians does seem to occur at critical stages of life, there are no rules, no obligatory, regular rites. Babies *may* be circumcised at birth, women *usually* undergo episiotomy during childbirth. We grow fat at puberty or during the menopause; my mother had her hair cut off when she was widowed; a neighbour insisted on having a hysterectomy during a difficult menopause although her doctor found no medical reason for it. Adolescents have their teeth pulled because fathers think their mouths are over-crowded. Cosmetic surgery often accompanies middle-aged status changes for men and women. A friend of mine, who at thirteen did not want to be parted from his mother by going off to boarding school, took to his bed and the doctor took out his appendix.

Psychologists maintain that there are profound psychological reasons for these mutilations, whether haphazardly performed among westerners or as part of institutionalized passage rites in other societies. Social anthropologists, studying cultures where life crises are often *celebrated* with surgery, maintain that there are profound social reasons: a traumatic experience involving the ordeal of pain and bodily transformation in the company of a group of peers creates a sense of security and confidence. The Black Australian body is used as a kind of icon, the cosmetic surgery that is part of the passage rite being accompanied by religious ceremonies and as boys become adolescents and girls women they become permanently aware of their new roles.

Among Black Australians the ritual moments are institutionalized: the individual as a member of the group accepts inevitable physical and social transformations. In this way Black Australians also come to terms with their physical selves – with their mouths, their genitals, their excrement, their blood – all aspects of the intimate body that reflect man's animal condition, a condition which men and women as 'cultured' human beings have always found unacceptable. The beastly body is mutilated by ritual experts and cosmetic surgeons so that it becomes human and so that it is no longer dangerous or alien.

Mutilation seems to work well for Black Australians who have precise rituals full of symbolic meaning, precise rules for precise status changes. For westerners, the mutilations – eccentric, unformalized actions – are insufficient to secure the body's dangerous orifices and alien boundaries, insufficient to turn the beast into a human being. Such actions reveal a desperate attempt by the individual to come to terms with himself; they are not rites incorporating him into adult and community life.

Part Four
Passage to Adulthood

Chapter Seven
Essences, Sacred and Profane

Baby into infant, infant into child, child into adolescent, adolescent into adult: the social transition of a child into an adult – through rituals usually accompanied by body alteration – is marked by important and elaborate Black Australian religious ceremonies. The most important of these are the initiation rites of adolescence when the youth is formally separated from the world of women, is marked physically (by circumcision, subincision and scarification) and psychologically (by a dramatic presentation of myths and accompanying subliminal shock). I am concerned here with the Black Australian rituals only insofar as the symbolic behaviour has meaning or parallels for White Australians and westerners. I am not going into ethnographical detail of the rites themselves nor am I attempting to explain the functions of these rites. Such details and explanations are fairly standard and can be found in a number of descriptive accounts.

Briefly, the major themes discussed by the anthropologists are birth and rebirth, ordeals, mutilation the sharing of sacred knowledge. In all the rites death and birth are simulated by initiated elders and neophytes. The mothers of the youths are told that their children have 'died', that the spirits have carried them off or killed them or eaten them. The initiates become babies who have to be taught everything over again by their elders. They learn to toddle and walk, to suckle and eat, to defecate cleanly. In fact the boys forget they were born by women – they are reborn by men, as men.

Anthropologists stress that the rites serve a social function in binding the community together, that the ceremonies strengthen the individual's sense of belonging. They point out that the hierarchical differences between generations, between fathers and sons, and uncles and nephews are emphasized. They note that the uncircumcised ignorant androgyne becomes a circumcised, educated adult who may now join the men in the sacred ceremonies, marry and have children. Psychological explanations of the rites shift the emphasis from the community to the individual. They propose that the removal of the foreskin symbolizes the final severing of the novice's umbilical connection with his mother; or that circumcision is a symbolic castration of the younger generation by the older; or that the subincision operation on the penis is an attempt by boys not to become men, but to become women, a symbolic expression of a universal male envy of the vagina or womb.

Initiation rites

The stages of the initiation rites are fairly similar throughout the Black continent. First, the novices are removed forcefully from wailing mothers and other females and painted with blood drawn from the arms and penises of the elders; some blood may be drunk. Second, the novices endure a period of seclusion and severe prohibitions, followed by tossing rites or fire rites, circumcision and the giving of presents. The fully initiated men take blood again and fasten feathers on their bodies to show the novices the totemic rites. The third stage is the ritual entry of the initiated youths into the main camp where they are welcomed by their close relatives. A fourth stage, often after the initiation rites proper, may include a further cutting of the penis (subincision) and cicatrization of the chest usually by the individual himself.

Almost all initiation rites, as van Gennep has shown, have similar patterns – the novices undergo seclusion, ordeals, rebirth, and instruction in sacred lore. African age-grade ceremonies, the jewish bar mitzvah, fraternal associations of western societies all follow this pattern. Freemasonry, for example, insignificant as its religious meaning may be, has all the characteristics of a primitive secret cult with a primitive emphasis on seclusion, ordeals and rebirth. There is an oath of secrecy that imposes death on the betrayer, secret passwords and signs. There are rites miming ordeals of death and rebirth, symbolic mutilations, ceremonies which relate a mythical history of the lodge. These rites, mumbo-jumbo to most of us, including myself, the son of a former lodge master, testify to a continuing delight in the kind of ceremony which, in Black Australian and American Indian society, we often mock.

If we accept the basic pattern of White and Black passage rites, whether they are weddings, funerals or initiation rites we shall have much less difficulty understanding the meaning of the Black Australian ceremonies. Let us look at some of the elaborate allegories and symbols of the Freemasons, although I should here warn the reader that my information is limited, since unlike White Australian anthropologists studying Black rites, I was never allowed the privilege of watching. The novice is sponsored by two members. He is told to undress (symbolic nakedness of the child): he removes his jacket and collar and tie and rolls up his left trouser leg above the knee. The shirt is opened to expose the left breast and the right shoe is removed and replaced by a slipper. The initiate is blindfolded in a hood (hoodwinked, secluded) and his death is symbolized by placing a noose around his neck. He then undergoes the ordeal: a confrontation with the Inner Guard who holds the point of a dagger at his bared breast. The initiate learns the symbols and the sacred signs, repeating ritual formulae to the worshipful master and swearing not to reveal, write, indite, carve, mark or engrave any of the secrets. Betrayal of these secrets involves the penalty of having 'his throat cut across, [his] tongue torn out by the roots and buried in the sand of the sea at low water mark, or a cable's length from the shore where the tide regularly ebbs and flows twice in twenty-four hours, or the more effective punishment of being branded as a wilfully perjured individual, void of all moral worth and totally inept to be received into this worshipful lodge.'

Black Australian initiation rites, being the core of their religion, have greater meaning for the society as a whole than the ritual antics of Freemasons. They have as profound a religious meaning and symbolic richness as christian rituals. Black ritual is an initiation into a religion that encompasses the whole of a person's life, and contributes to his and society's well-being, of the continuation of food resources and the natural environment, to the fertility of animals and human beings. A full description of these long rituals would present a complex cosmology, a panorama of attitudes to the natural world: to the stars and the planets, thunder and lightning, fire and natural catastrophes, the growth of animals and plants, seasonal changes, the relationships between men and women and between human beings and animals.

Whatever my anthropological generalizations, we must be in no doubt that the Black initiation rites are pure, profound religion. Christians practise a religion as well; but often it is a shadow of itself and some westerners exhibit more religious behaviour at a football match than in church and attribute more mana to a pop singer than to the Virgin Mary. During the initiation rites, Black novices, as well as being separated from the world of women and children – the profane world – are transformed by operation and ordeal and reintegrated into the sacred world. They begin to take part in religious activity that demonstrates order and continuity in society and the universe; they make offerings to the spirits and perform dances that perpetuate human life and animal species. The novices come into contact with totemic beings, spirits, gods, and in this way they are brought into a system that controls the Black Australian cosmos.

Those westerners fortunate enough to have the gift of religion are religious in exactly the same way as Black Australians. A churinga ceremony which takes place during the initiation rites can quite easily and quite properly be compared to the Stations of the Cross of a christian religious ceremony. In the christian communion rite the initiates contemplate the meaning of the life and death of Jesus – his trial by Pilate, the pietà, the taking down of the sacrificed body. Black initiates also watch their priest as he sits in a circle with a sacred churinga in his hands: geometrical figures represent the paths of the totemic ancestors; men sing and beat out the hymn while the priest sways in a religious trance, rubbing his thumb over the engraved lines to follow their spirit's movements.

Symbolism of rituals
There are of course differences. Christianity tends to stress

individual moral goodness and salvation. Black Australians emphasize life-giving and life-making elements. Their rituals are dedicated to the principles of life and fertility and therefore involve symbols of water, milk, fat, hair, blood and sexuality, and use intimate physical actions and body products. These elements of symbolic behaviour have a universal meaning and satisfy deep emotional and religious needs which no comparable ritual seems to do for westerners. It is important to remember that it is not the external sign that is important: it is not the actual 'blood' and 'flesh' (meat) of the christian rite or the ritual sodomy and violent physical actions of the Black ritual that are important, but rather what is being symbolized. These symbols reflect the fact that Black religion is concerned with life, and personalities are moulded by marking the body and the mind of the initiates with signs denoting aspects and stages of living.

Since Black religion emphasizes life and living, the symbols are frankly physiological: breasts and breast milk, menstrual blood and ordinary blood, male and female genitalia and their transformation or modification. In certain cases, semen, urine, excrement, copulation, and sodomy may become ritual symbols. Thus urine may be drunk; initiates may be born from the anuses of their elders and covered with excrement; their foreskins may be removed and eaten or saved to insert in the vulva of the bride. Blood may be drunk, used as an adhesive, painted on bodies; particular significance is given to penis blood. Of course there is nothing odd about a preoccupation with the body and sexuality in religion – it occurs in christianity – since it mirrors normal human physiological development and change.

Closely linked to body symbolism are the three universal colours: red, black and white, colours used symbolically in rituals throughout the world. They are universal not because of their ready availability or their brilliance or their rarity value. They are universal because they epitomize the main facts of human organic experience; they have explicit reference to the secretions and fluids and waste products of the body, and they have come to symbolize the three great moments of birth, life and death. They represent the three atavistic substances of the body and become symbols of basic drives. Red is blood, white is breast milk and semen, black is excrement. Rituals throughout the world use these colours to symbolize life-making, life-being and life-taking experiences, experiences of copulation and birth, growth and death. White–semen–breast milk is equated with birth and copulation; red–blood is equated with life; black–excrement with death. These are the world's three strong colours; yellows and greens and pale blues may be important at parties and in minor ceremonies. Red, black and white are the colours of the primary experiences of the body and are associated with the body's gratification of drives associated with sex, hunger, aggression and death and excretion.

This basic colour triad is used to represent and also to control the physical forces they represent. White is linked to purity and the mother–child tie; red is linked to reproduction, but also to bloodshed and hunting; black is linked with death and used as a symbol of death and of the transition from one state to another. In White Australia widows sometimes wear black; brides often wear white; normally neither would wear red. In other societies where virginity is not the aspect celebrated at weddings, red may be an appropriate colour for the bride as in the case of the ancient Romans or the modern Thais.

Despite my valiant attempts to dig them out, I found very little ritual exploitation of the triad of symbolic colours associated with body functions and excretions in White Australian culture. Nevertheless, in the west and particularly in Australia, much of religious symbolism seems to have been diverted to supposed trivialities such as food. White Australians have special attitudes to foods that, symbolically and through their shape, texture and colour, seem to express universal physiological functions. Milk and the once ubiquitous milk-bar represent the breast and infantile dreams; tomato sauce, Australia's second national drink, becomes a symbol of life, blood and the hunt, quite divorced from its origin in the humble tomato; vegemite, an odd concentrated symbol of black excrement, is spread on the early-morning toast as death wish and spiritual purgative. Perhaps White Australians should be credited with the invention of a fourth body symbol. Their sacred drink, the golden yellow beer, seems to represent urine and is commonly called 'piss' by the natives.

If I am to be accused of frivolity so be it: however before making the charge I should like you to think of examples of sacred food and sacred drinks that use silly colours such as pink or pale blue.

The basic human experiences of the body and of life, symbolized by this colour triad, are not exploited to the full in western religion; or if they are not they are hidden under layers of prudery and misunderstanding. We do not use semen, breast milk and excrement as part of our religious experiences, although certain christian sects take advantage of the immense symbolic meaning of blood. We have become oddly squeamish about many natural functions and body products. In most religions, blood, breast milk and excrement play an important role in ritual. In Ancient Greece animal and human faeces, breast milk, nail clippings, menstrual blood and urine were part and parcel of the rites.

I became dramatically aware of my own squeamish attitudes to blood – to life and death and their symbols – when I lived in the mountains of Cameroon in Africa. As part of my job and as part of my social position, I attended circumcision rites, childbirth, corpse-viewing, sacrifices, ritual autopsies. Regularly and to the great surprise of the people, I would faint, usually in the middle of a solemn ceremony; my friends attributed my disposition to 'die' to my spiritual sensitivity. I was also sprayed with the breast milk and invited to eat faeces: I did not faint though I felt squeamish. My main horror was of blood and I was advised by my academic superiors to spend a week or two in the surgical ward of a hospital in London before returning to the field. I continued to faint.

Blood, however, was once extensively used as a symbol in the western world, both as a magical element in religion and as a sign of continuity in social life. For the early Hebrews, blood was the suspension fluid of social life, the substance which enveloped the nomadic clan; we still use it to symbolize kinship relations – we even have blue blood.

Strangers who wished to join a Semitic tribe were inducted by means of a blood ritual, and blood-guilt that visited the father's sins on the children until the third or fourth generation figures in the old testament.

Blood for christians is still a magical symbol, as magical as blood for the Black Australians in their initiation rites. Blood, we also think, is a substance which is almost independent of the body: it was the blood of Abel the herdsman that 'cried out' for vengeance against the farmer-brother Cain. Unrelated friends who wished to become blood brothers drank each other's blood; they were then thought to have a part of each other's essence or being. And human blood is considered a magical element by modern peoples: during the Second World War, when the blood bank had too much blood, it was suggested in government circles that the excess blood should be made into blood puddings for general distribution on ration in Great Britain. However, the parliamentarians refused, viewing the consumption of human blood through the veins as one thing, and ingestion through the mouth as quite another.

By examining and accepting our own attitudes to blood, perhaps we can better understand Black Australian attitudes to this life-giving, magical substance. Blood is given to young men by older ones in order to strengthen the former. Blood drunk by initiates from the veins of the instructors is a symbolic transfusion of life. After a period of seclusion, the novice, naked, his eyes covered and his ears plugged, drinks a large quantity of human blood, and the older men come to him one by one and let blood flow from their veins on to his head. At the end of the ceremony the boy is anointed with blood and returns to the camp heralded by the noise of bull-roarers. During dances which tell the story of the travels of totemic animals, blood from either the penis or the basilic vein in the arm is sprinkled over the shoulders, chest and back of each dancer.

If we consider the magical role of the blood and flesh (meat) symbolism of holy communion we should be able to understand the symbolic role of blood in Black initiation rites. In the same way even excremental and phallic symbolism can be understood. During the initiation rites, since men give birth to young men anally, it is ritually appropriate that shit should accompany this male creation. The Greeks also covered male initiates with filth, in this case goat dung. In Ancient Greece and Black Australia, urine is drunk: men can not suckle babies after birth, so the Australians offer a symbolic substitute. We tend to draw back in horror from accounts of human excrement and urine being used in these ceremonies, forgetting that they are well-nigh universal religious symbols. During one period in the history of the christian church, the clergy at the Feast of Fools ate symbolic faeces in church and threw human ordure at the altar; until recently the Tibetans ground up the Grand Lama's faeces and made it into life-giving pills.

White Australians react with disgust and shock when they learn that the penis is used in religious rituals. We do not use human genitals as symbols in religious ceremonies but in christian ceremonies phallic symbols abound. I consider a phallic symbol to be an object which, because of its shape or its treatment as an extension of the human body (a gun or a spear), is considered powerful and ritually meaningful. In Black Australian rites, the symbol of virility is the spear which is normally used for hunting and fishing and killing people; White Australians have guns. The wooden sacred boards known as churinga are phallic symbols for Black Australians; White Australians have their surfboards. The latest male symbol in Australia is a new Sydney beer bottle, the 'hand-grenade' which combines the classical notion of the phallic shape, extension of the body, aggression and froth. I have never belonged to a fraternal lodge in Australia so I have no idea of their use of phallic objects. But I have visited the semi-secret, all-male ex-soldiers clubs: at one of them, next to the colour TV on the bar was a large hand-decorated chamber-pot with a huge painted pottery phallus poised amusingly above it. In another there was a rogues' gallery of members' portraits with the faces ingeniously formed of convoluted penises and testicles.

I am aware that I am not describing here the great symbols of a religion. Sometimes however these symbols do acquire

religious significance. African villages I visited had a monolith sunk into the ground – a stone phallus believed to contain
the power of dead chiefs and warriors; it was supposed to
rise up in the middle of the night, like an erect penis, and
protect the village from marauding witches and other evil
spirits. In anthropology we have no trouble writing that these
Africans used an explicit phallic symbol to protect them from
sorcery and witchcraft. It is difficult to accept such comments
when they are made about White Australian objects that
seem to have the same form and function. In Tasmania I
noticed that most towns had a war memorial with the names
of those killed during the two world wars. The form of the
memorial is frankly phallic and once a year the men of the
town perform sacred rites at dawn and spend the rest of the
day in a wild orgy of camaraderie and drinking. Yet I am
uneasy, even now, of writing that the Tasmanians have a
phallic monolith, sacred with the strength of male sacrifice,
which is thought to protect the town in the same way as the
penis-shaped stone in my African village.

Black Australians, unlike White Australians, are not shy
of celebrating sexuality and religion in the same symbol. The
most sacred of the churinga is the carved bull-roarer, an oval
board or stone which is rotated rapidly through the air and
as it spins gives out a weird, electrifying noise. The uninitiated – all women and children – believe that the amazing
sound of the bull-roarer is the voice of the totemic kangaroo,
but they never see it; if they did or were shown it by an
initiated man, the punishment for both would be death. Bull-
roarers are found at all secret male rites and as well as being
considered phalluses they are linked to thunder and wind.

The bull-roarer is defined in the *Concise Oxford Dictionary*
as a 'kind of noisy toy'and it is known in White Australia,
America and Europe as a child's toy: a small thin flat piece
of wood, usually oval with a hole in one end. In English it
has been called a roarer, a bull, a boomer, a buzzer, a whizzer
or a swish. Similar toys are still carried to football matches
and I have heard the dreadful shriek in Italian villages and
in the African bush. Black Australians believe that the spirit
represented by the bull-roarer dwells in wild and inaccess-

ible regions and only comes out when a youth is initiated. After circumcision the phallic spirit takes him away into the bush until he is better and can return as a circumcised, initiated man. At the end of the initiation the young men take back a miniature bull-roarer to the camp with them. During the initiation rites the bull-roarer seems to symbolize the growth of the novices from their ritual babyhood to adulthood. It is rubbed on the male organs of the young boys and the other participants form a ring and perform mutual masturbation.

Anthropologists have shown that the bull-roarer is not merely phallic in its symbolism, but through its association with thunder and wind is also linked to the anus and the passing of wind. During initiation rites, men run around with a bull-roarer, sometimes covered with excrement, frightening the novices as well as women and children outside the sacred ground. According to the interpretation by Alan Dundes, the bull-roarer becomes a farting phallus. The anthropologist presents a picture of men expressing themselves through the expulsion of air, trying to create life – futilely – by blowing through their anuses or making farting noises with objects such as the phallic bull-roarer.

This may sound like fun-ethnography. Even if it is, it is not fair to Black Australians to let White Australians off scot-free. I looked around for an important phallic symbol which seemed to fit all the requirements of the psychoanalyst and resembled the phallic, anal, flatulent bull-roarer: shape, extension of the body, power, cosmetic or aesthetic treatment, danger, noise. I did not have to look far.

Australia and the United States have the two greatest numbers of motor cars and drivers per capital of any country in the world. If the Black Australian's phallic symbols are his spear and his bull-roarer, the westerner's counterparts are his motor car and his motor bike. The real object for a Black Australian is the spear that he carries everywhere with him, held high in his right hand, ready to use, ready to kill; in drawings, the figure of a man holding a spear is also a sign for rape. The real object for a White Australian is the motor car that carries him everywhere, that is kept inside his house in a garage, like his penis behind his zip. The car is as important to him as his phallus: without it he would feel as naked as a Black Australian without his spear.

Spears and motor cars are like phalluses, especially as cars spurt forward and slow down, just as the penis becomes erect and then slackens. Motor cars are developed by their manufacturers not for their general practicability, but for their symbolic value – their longness, their streamlined shape, their 'thrustingness'. The motor car is painted and decorated, polished and smoothed like a part of the body; if we can't have a decorated (circumcised) penis at least we can have a decorated car. Motor cars are given names, pulled to pieces and greased. Why some people even put two round woolly cushions at the rear window! One White Australian carried his association with his car–penis to such an extreme that he invented a device so he could talk to it on the phone from a thousand miles away and make it go through its movements by remote control.

White Australians look after their cars with exaggerated care, usually on the holy day, Sunday. They are as terrified of an accident to their private cars as they are of injury to their private parts. An accident is a castration: a motor car is essential to the proud ethos of the maleness and without it a man is impotent and insignificant.

Very amusing. But, you warn, don't forget women drive cars. I know they do and for some women motor cars may even be phalluses. However on the whole, a little car is considered best for the little woman – hence, the ads stating 'lady's car'. In two-car families, the smooth, streamlined fast car with the quick get-away is suitable for the head of the house just as the spear is suitable for the Black Australian male. The slow family car is for the housewife; she carries the shopping and the children and the family dog, just as the Black woman carries the domestic loads – her babies, her baskets and digging stick.

Like spears, motor cars kill: a very un-phallic-like activity in one sense since the penis should be considered the agent of birth not death. About four thousand Australians are killed on the roads each year. Drunken drivers run down the unwary and the old with their substitute iron phalluses and become impotent wrecks when the judge takes away their licence to drive/kill. Yet multi-million dollar industries continue being constructed around this phallic killer; large areas of Australian towns have been razed for new super highways, people have been ejected from their homes, and public lands and parks have been taken over. If phallic behaviour is necessary I prefer it confined to religious rites even if it does involve mutual masturbation, sodomy and penis mutilation.

Chapter Eight
Gender Identity

Western societies, along with many others, do not have initiation at puberty. There may be obvious reasons why a society based on individualistic capitalism should deny adolescents formal and public rituals at this critical time. For the individual, however, it means that he must come to terms with the problems of sexuality and growing up alone. Instead of ritual, we have disturbed teenagers and infantile adults. We have groups and fashions, bodgies and widgies, the teds and the punk rock, the drug culture. Of course young White Australians can be confirmed and take a driving licence, have twenty-first birthdays and tattoo their biceps. But no society-wide symbolic religious experience makes them men or women; the state steps in pragmatically. Whether or not young men and women have been circumcised, grown a beard, married and mothered or fathered children, at the age of eighteen they are magically and officially converted into adults. They can now elect governments, enter the sacred precincts of bars, legally kill people as soldiers. Overnight the juvenile delinquent becomes a criminal, a wayward girl a whore.

During the Black initiation rites, when the older men circumcise the novices, isolated cases of sodomy and ideas concerning the symbolic birth of the initiates through the anuses of the elders have given rise to some wild generalizations about castration complexes, the Oedipus complex, and homoerotic behaviour. As far as the homosexual behaviour is concerned, the participants insist that the behaviour makes the boys 'grow'. White observers may suggest that it sublimates the boys' unconscious feminine desires. I believe that the explanations are complex: sex between men during the rites may involve vagina envy, homoerotic tendencies, castration associated with a universal Oedipus complex, a symbolic attempt to separate boys from the world of women, and an aggressive display of the ranking superiority of the elder generation.

One thing ritual sodomy is *not* is an example of 'guilty pederasty': homosexuality in the context of ceremonial behaviour is symbolic action. For example, in the context of hierarchical behaviour between generations, sex between active men and passive adolescents is a demonstration of the political and moral power of 'fathers' over their 'sons'. Subordinate males become females because the female sexual role is the submissive one. We have already seen that male primates, including humans, mature more slowly than females and that adulthood for them is a social rather than physical event. The initiation rites which create a socially mature Black Australian male may last up to ten years; during that time the 'children' are prepared for adult 'genitality' and marriage by learning sexual taboos, having their penises circumcised and being purified, through ritual, of the defilement of women. Initiation not only proves to the world that a man has acquired totemic secrets, it also shows that he has overcome child-like (and woman-like) urges, and he can then join the ranks of adult men and marry in order to have children. As proof of his social adulthood, he is given the right to wear the special clothing of manhood: forehead bands and feather plumes, face-markings of red and white ochre and decorative belts and tassels, necklaces fashioned of pearl shell and kangaroo teeth.

While the boys live with women, they are classified with women. During the rites, the boys are 'grown up' again by men, reborn through their anuses into the world of Men and Culture. As part of this process the novices must learn to respect and fear the power of the old men of their clan and the new obedience of the youth is in strong contrast to the unbridled independence and unruly temper of the uninitiated boy.

Ritual sodomy, therefore, is a means of impressing on the boys the political power of their elders. Since it seems that males become physically mature long before they become socially mature, ritual serves to delay the moment when young men can form permanent unions with women. Even in non-human primate society, the young males of a troop are kept off the females by devious means. Males are sexually active long before their elders give them a position in the troop sexual and social organization; the young males of a troop of apes could obviously kill their older relatives and take over political power and the women. Non-human and human primates achieve political and social dominance partly by sexual aggression. When male baboons mount each other it is not homosexuality, but rank behaviour. Aggression between older and younger primate males is ritualized and the aggression of the young is directed away from their elders, often towards an external foe. Among hamadyas baboons, young males even develop red backsides like females on heat, which they use in a social rather than a sexual context; they display like meek young females to superior males. And as females, the young males are tolerated and not harmed by the powerful, jealous older males.

Human beings also use sexual signals in social situations. In initiation rites when we find an insistent attention to the anus, male parturition and homosexuality, we must look for the symbolic function of ritual sexual activity. Menstruation and childbirth are acted out in symbolic terms by men and heterosexual intercourse is rejected temporarily in favour of homosexuality. When a Black Australian boy leaves the world of women to join the world of men he finds that in the process of becoming a man he may have to pretend to be a woman; in other words he has his masculinity challenged by being made to serve as the passive sexual object of an older male.

Black elders are determined to enjoy the pleasures of middle age, and so grant adolescents some of the prerogatives of adulthood, but not all of them at once. White elders clumsily do the same thing by controlling economic resources, political power and women. They regulate through government ordinance the legal age of maturity; they send the young men off to wars for long periods; they extend infantile behaviour by excessively prolonged schooling and dependence on the older generation. There is no universal rite of sodomy although such sexual aggression is implicit in many initiation rites involving new recruits to the army and military service, new inmates in prisons and new boys at public schools. The younger men may be made to serve as the passive sexual objects of older males. Sexuality in these cases is linked to submission.

Men's envy of women

As well as being buggered, the Black novices are also born to the older men. During the rites, the initiates die and are reborn; when reborn, they are informed of the mysteries, the myths, the true names of the totemic spirits, the reality behind the sound of the bull-roarer. The novices die and become embryos in the paternal rather than the maternal womb, in the darkness of cultural rather than natural creation. The novices first imitate the behaviour of the dead and then new-born babies. Circumcision is an external mark of death and a painful mutilation symbolic of parturition.

Rebirth, naturally enough, is expressed through basic body symbolism: the boys are being born from the anuses of the men in a special enclosure known as 'the place of excrement'; bull-roarers roar and the boys are made to eat shit, symbolically becoming foetus–excrement as they pass through the bodies of their elders. The men transform the natural babies into cultural men by a graphic and dramatic representation of labour, birth and feeding. In the Kunapipi rites, for example, the novices are painted with red ochre and blood and taken to a sacred ground where the main ritual takes place in a trench or symbolic uterus. The men emulate women's procreative powers by making their genitals bleed in a simulation of the menstrual flow.

Now this is ritual rebirth and for some commentators it has been seen as frank vagina or womb envy.* Men attempt to rival women's natural procreative powers through the

---

*My discussion of the relationship of vagina envy and male initiation derives initially from Bruno Bettelheim's insights in his book *Symbolic Wounds: puberty rites and the envious male* (New York, Collier, 1962) and Alan Dundes' article, 'A psychoanalytic study of the bullroarer', *Man*, Vol. II, No. 2, 1976.

symbolism of excrement, birth, sodomy, menstruation. In the rites men try to look like women, act as women, become women. Since Freud we have become accustomed to the idea of female penis envy, associated with the male's contempt of the female because she has no penis. Women have always revealed their envy of the dominant sex by dressing as men, performing men's roles. They have been able to express a natural penis envy simply because males smugly expect to be envied. Vagina envy has no such obvious outlets: when White Australian men dress as women, putting on skirts and flowered hats, they are ostracized, mocked and even thrown into prison. Lesbianism is legally tolerated but homosexuality between males is a crime.

White Australian men may be expected to have a basic envy of women in their femininity and reproductive capacities, but they are not allowed to express it. In Black initiation rites a covert envy of women's creative powers finds an outlet in ritualized birth by males and by ritualized sodomy. Subincision too is an expression of this envy.

In the subincision operation the penis is supposed to become like a vulva with a permanent vagina-like aperture. Subincision occurs some time after circumcision and the main initiation ritual. The expert makes a slit through the ventral surface of the organ into the urethra, from the orifice to a position about an inch along the shaft. Often this cut is extended, bit by bit, by the individual himself until the full extent of the penile urethra is converted into an open channel. The operation is done without ceremony, the significance of the mutilation appearing during the community ceremonies when the subincised men pierce these incisures so that when they dance blood splashes on to their thighs, on to the sacred objects and on to the novices. It is interesting to note that in mythology there are frequent references to animals with subincised penises. Among the very odd fauna of the Australian continent grooved penises are common: the kangaroo, the possum and the emu all have double or bifurcated gland penises like the subincised Black Australian.

The ethnographical evidence seems to suggest that the

subincised penis is considered an imitation vulva, not an imitation kangaroo or emu penis. The wounded penis in some parts of Australia is actually called 'vulva' and the bleeding that occurs when the operation is repeated during ceremonies is likened to women's menstruation. In many societies outside Black Australia 'male menstruation' is regarded as female behaviour: it is a kind of purification, blood-letting occurring at regular intervals in order to maintain general good health by losing bad, polluting blood. In Black Australian groups, the food taboos associated with subincision and menstruation are exactly the same. Initiation, through subincision, therefore, does seem to change men into women as well as into higher-status men. In acquiring a vulva-like opening to the penis and in repeated genital bleeding the men express their bisexuality; women, say the men, are already bisexual since they are born with a clitoris.

Black Australians express their femaleness in symbolic ways, freeing themselves from anxiety about their sex and from the universal subconscious desires to possess female organs, functions and birth experience. They frankly accept during the ceremonies the important role of female functions in their emotional lives. When the men masturbate together, have homosexual intercourse, eat shit, have babies, they are living and procreating as men–women in a dream world without women.

All aspects of the initiation rites are carried out in secret, of course. Engaging in acts normally performed by the despised female race must, at all costs, be kept from them; revelation of such behaviour would reduce the proclaimed superiority of males to a shallow sham. This subject of vagina envy is linked to the couvade and the Black Australian dogma of virgin birth discussed earlier. The less the Black Australian understands or says he understands of the masculine role in conception, the more he will want to assert his role as 'mother' during initiation. Since women create human life, men have created ritual so they can procreate spiritually and symbolically. Totemic rites are performed to maintain a supply of animals and plants; because children are intimately connected with totemic species, such rites are also concerned with the creation of human spirits. Male obsession with ritual is a compensation for the fact that their world depends on women who create life.

Perhaps this interpretation of some of the symbolism of Black initiation rites puts a different complexion on the western view of the position of Black women. According to certain myths, women once owned everything, including the sacred objects and ceremonies. One day the men stole them and when the mythical sisters found their ritual paraphernalia gone, they accepted the situation philosophically: let the men carry on the tedious business of the ritual while they busied themselves with the important business of raising families and collecting food. Women as a result were forbidden to know the mysteries and ceremonies involving ritual bloodshed – just as western women are banned from men's secret fraternities, the inner sanctums of ex-soldiers' clubs and denied full participation in christian rites. In the past women not dedicated to virginity had to sit in a special part of the church and could not even approach the altar because they were considered polluting. They were not allowed in the choir to sing sacred songs; male castrati sang the highest parts. Although the Catholic priest is ambiguously dressed in women's clothes, White women may not become priests.

Masculine and feminine

It is only recently that White Australians have begun to understand the lack of rigidity and the ambiguity of sexual roles. Black Australians are not behaving eccentrically or very exotically when they reject clear-cut male and female roles. In the animal world, a merging of male and female roles and even a confusion of physical organs is commonplace, and human males have useless nipples while women have useful clitoris–penises. In some animal species the similarity between the sexes is extraordinary: spotted hyena males and females are hardly distinguishable. The external organs are similar and the female even has two visible scrotum pouches immediately under the anus and a penis like the male's. As we have seen among non-human primates, female physical attributes and behaviour are often imitated by males: young male baboons have oestrus swellings and imitate female rutting signals – they use the female invitation to copulation as a greeting to an older and superior male.

Myths found throughout the world reveal that originally, man was thought to be biologically androgynous. In the Kunapipi rite for example, the subincised penis is said to represent both the mythical Rainbow Serpent and the incisure of the Great Mother, indicating a coincidence of masculine and female symbols in the original phallus. Even Adam seems to have been a hermaphrodite since Eve was removed from his body. Black Australian rites recognize that men feel a need to express their femininity and women their masculinity. In the male initiation rites there is an attempt to repeat the bisexual unity of the mythical androgyne.

White Australians on the other hand theoretically follow a 'myth' of the pure male and the pure female, a myth based on a misguided belief in an exaggerated sexual differentiation. The process of becoming adult and all-male or all-female in White Australia means that children must rid themselves as far as possible of those tendencies that 'culture' has arbitrarily ascribed to the other sex. This refusal to accept a degree of bisexuality is so extreme that it results in bitter sexual antagonism and a neurotic belief in the superiority of one or the other sex. Occasionally the deep-seated desire to play the role of the other sex is revealed: young children dress up in cross-sex clothing and there is a hint of sexual rebellion in the fancy dress at New Year's Eve, during carnival time and at Halloween when the old become young, men become women and girls become boys for a certain time. Wearing a dress for one day, someone once said to me, teaches a man more about himself than wearing trousers and a shirt and a tie every day of his life.

White Australian men no doubt envy women their physique and their reproductive capacities, but they do not resolve personal sexual conflict through the ritualization of vagina envy as do Black Australians in their initiation rites. Do westerners ever have the desire to imitate the female genitalia, menstruation and pregnancy? Psychoanalysts working mainly in America, have shown that among adolescents, particularly disturbed adolescents, tensions do occur around the problem of the physical differences between the sexes. One group of adolescents expressed these tensions by inflicting wounds on their penises, emphasizing bleeding, which gave them feelings of sexual success and pleasure. These modern adolescents shared with Black Australians the need to suffer physical pain as the price of adult sexuality and the desire to imitate the bleeding of the female genitalia at menstruation. It would be wrong to equate the actions of neurotic children and adult Black Australians, as religious rituals cannot be viewed as an attempt to solve personal psychological problems. On the other hand, it may be true that the disturbed person who mutilates his penis and envies menstruation is a normal person exaggerated. Moreover we should not underestimate the emphasis on ritual rebirth in initiation rites throughout the world: rebirth by men seems to reflect a basic vagina envy.

If vagina envy is as universal a complex as penis envy and if, as Freud insisted, pure masculinity and femininity are not to be found either in a psychological or biological sense, how do rigidly sexed White Australians, particularly males, deal with the problem? Their persistent envy of female capacities to enjoy a primal creative experience by giving birth and their own submerged femininity are often expressed in so-called normal activities such as excessive beer-drinking, an obsession with the breast and homoerotic behaviour associated with the cult of mateship. Although White Australians are not in the habit of mutilating their penises, any hospital nurse will tell you that tattooed penises are common. Freudians have noted that other parts of the body are phallus substitutes: the ear, the hair, the nose; intentional wounding, piercing, and cosmetic surgery are often performed on erogenous zones which are phallus substitutes. It has been suggested that tattooing with its spectacular loss of blood may be an unconscious attempt to duplicate some of the natural features of female menstruation. Apparently male blood donors always outnumber women; psychoanalysts have suggested that this blood giving reveals a deep need on the part of men to sustain a loss of blood as women do at menstruation.

Womb envy is as common as vagina envy among

disturbed young men, perhaps once again demonstrating the behaviour of normal men, exaggerated. The desire to become pregnant is found among adolescents in mental hospitals; the boys imagine themselves pregnant, and overeat and develop a protruding stomach and even the stance and gait of a pregnant woman. Normal White Australian men practise a unique form of body mutilation that may imitate pregnancy. As the result of an excessive and obsessive amount of beer-drinking, the bodies of young men may assume the proportions of a pregnant woman. Dressed up in the national costume – shorts and heeled shoes which push out the buttocks and show off the bellies – the men look like females heavy with child. I once listened to a dinkum ocker middle-aged White Australian father ranting at his son for being an effeminate wastrel. (Here I must immediately declare an interest since as a boy and young man I was frequently told not to be a cissy, a poofter, a pansy or a fairy but to be a 'real' man.) The father pointed a scornful beringed finger at the long hair, beard, earrings and dirty jeans of his adolescent son. Now leaving aside the fact that none of these attributes are particularly womanly, let us look at the supposedly all-male father. He sat fatly in a deck-chair wearing bright red brogues with a fringed tongue, lemon-coloured socks up to his knees, a pair of bottle-green shorts which only barely covered his erogenous thighs, with a patent leather belt and gold-engraved buckle, and a floral shirt of greens, blues and yellows: a very colourful bird indeed. His son was a cissy because he had a beard and dirty trousers; the father was a man all right, mate, because he was clean-shaven like a woman and his hair had been cut short and had a vaginal-virginal central parting.

Far-fetched? Maybe. But not any more so than the theories expounded by psychoanalysts and anthropologists studying Black Australian ethnography. Gender identity clearly presents a problem for both the Black and the White Australian man; neither can be sure at times whether he's Arthur or Martha. Black Australians solve the problem with ritual and psychological finesse but they live in a world where the division of labour between the sexes is clear-cut and where role-changing is not occurring. In the west the problem of uncertainty is exacerbated by a general tendency for males to move towards female roles; the opposite trend – females moving towards male roles – is far less pervasive despite the women's liberation movement.

In some cases the changes towards a more feminine male identity are spectacular. Men are becoming much more involved in the domestic and natural world of childbirth and housework once considered the exclusive domain of wives and female relatives. Society is becoming feminized: men show an increased interest in such traditionally feminine things as cosmetics, purses, pierced ears, jewellery, the hairdresser; there is no longer as much stress on the all-male apprenticeships of drinking with the boys on Saturday night – or every night – or of being drafted along with their age-mates.

It is time, of course, that vagina envy was made respectable, like penis envy. In the past, our male-oriented society has forced boys and men to repress their feminine side; the repression of the masculine side of girls and women has been less severe. Trends towards accepted behaviour that dramatizes men's envy of women as menstruators and childbearers can only be advantageous. Men might then become less enthusiastic about noisy motor bikes, fast cars and war, and might openly acknowledge their urge to create life.

Black Australian rites give dramatic expression to basic drives and desires which, if freely manifested in western society, would be considered deviant to say the least. Instead of repressing vagina envy, womb envy and bisexuality, Black Australians with infinite if unconscious wisdom recognize their existence and provide ritual outlets for the tensions. They do not dress up as women all their lives; nor do they indulge in mutual masturbation or sodomy once happily married. Might it not be better for the White Australian male psyche if men went through a kind of initiation rite whereby they could eat symbolic shit and urine, dress up as girls, be buggered once and for all, and act out a symbolic pregnancy and parturition? In one fell blow, subconscious drives and fears would be dramatized and resolved.

Part Four
Passage to Parenthood

Chapter Nine

Marriage

Black Australians marry in order to have children, economic partners, and brothers-in-law. Once upon a time western people married to have legitimate sex and legitimate children; christian marriage, bastion of the christian family, was a legal and holy union sanctified by the state and the church. Nowadays people can get sex without marrying, are happy to father or mother bastards, are indifferent to the christian sacraments – but they are marrying more than ever. Even when they get divorced, they don't divorce to get unmarried: they divorce because one or both of the partners want to remarry. What is the fascination of marriage for White Australians, Americans, Europeans who have no religious, economic, legal, emotional imperatives to do so?

Rights and obligations

Marriage, of course, is not simply a religious or legal institution that legalizes sex and legitimizes children; it is a bundle of disparate rights and obligations. Let us look at the functions and progress of Black Australian marriage to see if we can understand our own fragile but apparently indomitable institution.

A Black Australian would say that he marries in order to have children and rights over these children; he is so anxious to marry that he submits to the long initiation rites and bodily mutilation that are prerequisite to his taking a wife. His betrothal may even occur before his future wife is born – when he claims the daughter of an accredited mother-in-law. Once married his aim is to have male and female children, the former to look after him in old age and his ghost in death, and the latter to serve as pawns in the political game of marriage. There are no illegitimate Black Australian babies since a woman is 'married' before she can conceive and is

automatically remarried when her husband dies. The only
way for a Black child to be a bastard would be if the husband
refused to perform the paternal ritual after its birth; but as
Black Australians are indifferent to physiological as opposed
to spiritual paternity, such rejection is only hypothetical. As
far as westerners are now concerned, I do not think a definition of marriage would specify the procreation of children
and their legitimization as an essential part of the marriage
contract; yet such a condition holds for most of the peoples
of the world. Curiously, although Catholic doctrine main-
tains that sexuality is only for procreation, annulment of an
unconsummated marriage involves sex, not specifically children.

Black Australians marry to have children, not to have sex,
although marriage gives them sexual rights to each other;
as in White Australia sexual rights are unequal – only the
woman is expected to sacrifice her body entirely to the
spouse. White Australians did once marry for sexual opportunities; christian marriage, with its insistence on premarital
chastity, virginity and marital fidelity, is – or was – a very
rare case of marriage as a licence for sex.

In Black Australia marriage is a complex social institution,
not a biological convenience. Marriage sets up important
relations between groups, between the clans of wives and
the clans of husbands; a man often marries to have an influential father-in-law or a brother-in-law as a friend or ally.
This aspect of marriage as an alliance is no longer stressed
in western marriage except between wealthy or aristocratic
families. Marriage gives a Black Australian access to his
wife's labour and vice versa; the contract helps them gain
a livelihood and the pronounced division of labour between
men and women means that it is an economic necessity to
marry; collectors of vegetable foods (females) join forces
with hunters and warriors (males). In White Australia the
union of symbolically complementary roles is becoming less
and less important and few couples would admit to marrying
in order to acquire a provider (male) or a domestic slave
(female).

Marriage cannot be said to provide sexual opportunities

for Black Australians as they are allowed promiscuity from an early age. But while they may not marry for sex, they certainly have sex. Marriage for the Black husband, as for the White husband, means that he no longer needs to go out looking for sex every night. Permanent mating among animals and human beings seems to serve the same purpose: sexual partners need not search for each other again and again. Interestingly, neither animals that have permanent mates nor most married humans have display dress. Marriage seems to supplant this need for the striking displays that birds, fish and animals that must attract casual mates have developed.

Do westerners marry out of economic self-interest – in other words for security, money? In Black Australia since there is no concept of accumulation of individual or communal property – apart from a few personal possessions – marriage provides no opportunity for capital gains. On the other hand, in White Australia people do – or did – marry for economic security, and marriage laws once provided for a legal division of property should there be a divorce. Nowadays, however, individuals often prefer to keep their private property private; wives and husbands have separate bank accounts, separate stores of wealth, sometimes even separate homes so that in the event of divorce there are fewer complications.

Ceremony

It is clear that Black Australians have solid reasons for getting married: they marry to have a legitimate spouse and legitimate children, to have useful in-laws, to achieve adult status. Why do White Australians insist on legalizing sexual unions? Emotional satisfactions, personal happiness are now placed above considerations of property, family, children, in-laws. White Australians say they marry for love, for emotional security, to escape their parents. None of these explanations is sufficient for the sociologist. I believe that marriage is a deep, universal imperative for human beings in society, an imperative involving a basic need for ritualization or ceremonialization of a basic passage rite. The problem here is to discover which passage rite the modern sacraments of marriage celebrate. It is not the passage rite into sex or into parenthood: it is the passage rite into adult maturity which begins in early adolescence for Black Australians but which is unnaturally delayed for White Australians – and for many perpetually denied.

For Black Australians the great passage rite is initiation at adolescence. For White Australians the wedding ceremony seems to fill this function. Westerners are marrying more and more and younger and younger and it seems that many of them marry simply in order to get away from mum and dad, set up house and become grown-up. Marriage is an initiation into one aspect of adulthood and this has always been so. A bachelor is a half-person, a 'child'. A spinster is to be pitied even more – not because she has been left on the shelf sexually or because she has no children, but because the status of being un-married has always been considered a second-class status, the wifely role defining a worthy woman. People marry to be married, to undergo the basic ceremonies of a passage rite. For this reason the White Australian and American marriage ceremony has always been relatively elaborate. Black Australian marriage despite its social significance for the community is nowhere thought worthy of the splendid rites and religious symbolism that are found in the initiation rites. Like some White Australians, they sometimes marry with no ceremony at all. Unlike White Australians, however, they believe that the great passage rites are those of adolescence–adulthood and those of death; the moment of marriage is of lesser significance.

Nevertheless as a passage rite, weddings are celebrated by most of the peoples of both groups. For both Black and White Australians, marriage involves a kind of sacrament, a rite of solemn engagement involving an important change of status. Usually the Black bride and groom leave the camp for a day or two; they return covered with festive red ochre and the girl's parents give them presents. As in all passage rites, the individuals move through a number of transitional states each marked by a ceremonial enactment. In the traditional White Australia, the early stages of courting and engagement are preparatory rites; when wedding and honeymoon are over, the individuals emerge as a married couple with a new home, a new set of relatives and friends and, for the woman at least, a new name. My claim is that even with the withering away of traditional christian ceremonies, the basic ritual stages – separation, transition and reincorporation into society – are always made. This is true when a couple marries in a Hindu temple, a registry office, naked on the beach in front of a few friends or in prison. The empty ritual of a church wedding or the improvised party and goings-on of a casually celebrated sexual liaison share elements found in marriage ceremonies and other passage rites throughout the world and throughout history.

In both Black and White Australian societies the status change of marrying occurs in stages, often clearly marked. At the end of the first stage, for example, the White couple may exchange engagement rings. They then purchase a licence or call the banns. Then comes some kind of ceremony; the final stage is the honeymoon, followed by the symbolic lifting over the threshhold of a new home. This process may last years, months or a few days in White Australia. In Black Australia it can take almost a lifetime.

Marriage for Black woman may begin, as we know, before she is born. For a man it may be said to begin when he is circumcised. His circumcisor often belongs to a category of relatives from which he may take a wife. Circumcision by a 'father-in-law' is usually a public indication that a particular group will one day provide the boy with a wife; 'one day' – since in gerontocratic Black Australia men rarely have a chance of marrying until they are nearly thirty. Here we already have a dramatic parallel between a 'primitive' rite and a ceremony found in our own cultural traditions. The Hebrew words 'circumcisor' and 'father-in-law' are so closely related linguistically that it is probable that the same term once designated both roles and that in circumcising a male child, a man was offering him his daughter as a future wife.

However in Black Australia, there is all the difference in the world between having a 'father-in-law' and having a wife or even a mother-in-law. All Black Australians have, from an early age, complete knowledge of the field of eligible spouses. In marrying there are special rules to follow: the simplest system is that children of brothers and sisters continually remarry over generations; this is known as bilateral cross-cousin marriage. The more common marriage is one between a man and his mother's mother's brother's daughter's daughter. In our society this relative is a special type of second cousin; in Black Australia all these female 'second cousins' are called 'wife' because they are potential wives – daughters of all the men a man calls 'father-in-law' and sisters of his 'brothers-in-law'. Thus a certain group of women marries a certain group of men, and a man uses the same term for the women he does marry eventually and any he might marry.

For a White Australian, this system of structured marriage prospects smacks of arranged marriages and is anathema to the ideas of individual choice and personal happiness. The Black Australian system means that girls marry the men their fathers or other relatives find for them. As in most societies where mated pairs are the basic units of ordered society, Black Australians believe that the stability of marriage should not be disturbed by the vagaries of personal inclination and romantic love. For them, marriage is not a romantic union between individuals; they marry for many reasons, but certainly not for love!

In some Black societies marriage is almost a politico-commercial undertaking. After initiation a circumcised man must persuade his titular 'father-in-law' to give him rights to one of his 'daughters': an important man with a large family distributes his daughters – born and unborn – as favours to friends and relatives, using the females as capital assets. A man will choose a son-in-law for his ability as a hunter so that he may have another able young man to look after him in old age; or he may prefer a political alliance with a powerful man who is already married. The system may be played to the advantage of husbands and in-laws. A go-ahead young man may succeed in finding several fathers-in-law ready to invest their daughters in him so that by the time he is thirty, when most of his age-mates are still bachelors, he may find himself the happy husband of several girls. The boy must interest himself in his distant future at an early age, attempting to control events that will not come to fruition for many years. While waiting for his wives to be born and grow, he has love affairs and perhaps a formal homosexual relationship. He may be fortunate enough to inherit an old widow, past child-bearing age, but not past other wifely duties.

The first major ceremonial concerned with the long process of marriage is called by anthropologists 'mother-in-law' bestowal, in many ways a misnomer since what are actually bestowed are rights to a woman's daughter or daughters. These rights are controlled – or 'owned' – by her (the mother-in-law's) husband. A young man is presented by his 'father-in-law' cum circumcisor cum 'mother's mother's brother' to his future mother-in-law. She may be only a young girl of five or six – because of the scarcity value of women in polygynous Black Australia, a mother-in-law is usually younger than her son-in-law. Even before she is cohabiting with her husband, the fruit of her womb is promised to a son-in-law. The future wife is already bestowed as a wife to another because *her* mother was bestowed as a mother-in-law. Since all girls become mothers-in-law in this way, men compete for mothers-in-law rather than for wives.

As far as the girl herself is concerned, being a mother-in-law means that she has a faithful friend and servant to look after her and bring her presents of useful objects and food. We must remember that when a young man has a girl bestowed on him as mother-in-law, he gains sexual rights to her daughter, never to the mother-in-law despite the fact that she is much younger than him. Since most Black Australian communities are organized in dual divisions, known as moieties, which are intermarrying groups, a man has 'wives' in one moiety and 'mothers-in-law' in the other – his own – and they are therefore tabooed sexually.

This explains the strict avoidance rule between mothers-in-law and their sons-in-law. Once circumcised, a man can not approach or speak to or deliberately look at a 'mother-in-law'. He must be discreet in her presence and never share food with her. If he sees a woman approaching who is in his 'mother-in-law' category of relatives, he must turn and run away from her presence, even if she is a toddler playing with other children. The taboo therefore applies to all women – mother's mother's brother's daughter's daughters, or cross-cousins – who could become his wife through normal marriage or widow inheritance. If a man sees foot-prints in the sand and knows they are his mother-in-law's he erases them with his foot. During ceremonies men usually face in one direction and women in another; the men sing and the women dance in a group behind them, avoiding each other as groups since every woman is bound to have a son-in-law or a potential son-law among the men.

The avoidance of a woman and her son-in-law is not aimed solely at proscribing sexual unions. It is symbolic behaviour which reflects the importance of the in-law relationship, the alliance of groups which exchange wives. Avoidance is a means of showing respect; the mother-in-law is the most important person in a man's life, his best-friend, and if he avoids her, he avoids quarrels which may endanger this friendship and hence his marriage prospects.

The in-law relationship is often a delicate one in White Australian society as well. At a wedding the kin of the bride and groom sit on opposite sides of the church and treat each other gingerly, if at all, during the reception. The post-marriage relationship of mothers-in-law and their sons-in-law and daughters-in-law is set off from other relationships by subtle gradations of behaviour and etiquette even years after the marriage; mothers-in-law are treated formally. Innocent customs such as the old taboo on lifting a teapot in another woman's home or poking the fire in the hearth reflect the need for a proper role assignment between visiting parents-in-law and their children's spouses. In White Australia, married couples insist on a fresh, independent start – in fact they often marry just for that – and the mother-in-law, internationally a difficult relative, needs special treatment if she is not to wreak havoc. Mother-in-law jokes in the west reflect the same difficulties mitigated by the avoidance relationship found among Black Australians.

A Black Australian's marriage prospects look up when his mother-in-law becomes pregnant, only to be dashed if the child is a boy. Sometimes, he compensates for this tragedy by considering his brother-in-law a kind of surrogate wife. When a girl is born, his hopes are realized. When she is about nine, the girl begins to visit her husband. At first the husband, usually old enough to be her father, treats her as a daughter, holding her on his lap, giving her tidbits of meat and fondling her. He keeps his girl-wife especially well-greased with fat to make her grow. The girl learns her wifely role by accompanying the women of her husband's group when they collect firewood and water, usually under the care of her mother-in-law or her husband's first wife if he is already married.

Marriage for Black Australians is therefore a gradual process, the first move occurring before she is born and the last when she is 'raped' by a special group of men appointed by her husband. In some cases there is no precise moment, no specific ceremony when the couple is married. Usually, both mother and father must agree to the girl's moving in with her husband. Sometimes a girl of ten or eleven will simply be taken across to another fire one night and told: 'You sleep here now with your husband.' In White Australia, there is a definite moment – either legal or sacred – when most marriages may be said to be formalized: from the moment the ring is slipped on the finger and a document is signed, the couple is married and sexual consummation follows. In traditional western marriage when sexual rights and virginity were all-important, great symbolic attention was given to the 'moment of marriage'. Modern marriage seems to be assimilating the gradual nature of the Black marriage system; formal marriage can now be preceded by a period of trial marriage and even the birth of children.

Although Black Australians do not mark the 'moment of marriage' with the elaborate ceremonial and religious symbolism of the initiation rites, their marriage celebrations have features common to weddings all over the world. Weddings usually involve feasting, dancing, dressing up, sexual initiation, moral instruction, a form of contract, an exchange of gifts, a symbolic ceremony. Rings are exchanged, hands are entwined, fertility cakes are eaten or distributed. The ceremony varies from people to people: in the traditional christian wedding the couple becomes 'one flesh' for life through the magical action of the holy sacraments; the man and woman were entitled, and expected, to share a hotel room from then on, beginning during their honeymoon, an intrinsic part of the White Australian ceremony; it was assumed they would become parents shortly.

Because wedding ceremonies seem to have a common symbolism whether they happen in Arnhem Land or All Saints, Newtown, a description of wedding ritual always seems to strike a familiar note. In ancient Rome the bride had her hair imprisoned in a veil and wore a special bridal dress secured around the neck with a metal collar. In those days, before pre-marital virginity was so prized, the colour of the dress was red. She stood with her family and welcomed the groom and her relatives; there was a sacrifice to the gods after which witnesses sealed the marriage contract. The couple exchanged vows and rings and the guests burst into loud congratulation. The bride was wrenched from her mother's weeping embrace and 'raped' (carried off by force) to her husband's home where she was lifted across the threshold. In ancient Rome, and Black and White Australia, the important elements of a passage rite recur: there is always the idea of retreat, emergence and stepping or being carried into a new life. Black Australians share ceremonial food, retire to the bush for a day or two and return covered with red ochre. In White Australia rings are exchanged, a fertility cake is consumed, the mother cries, the guests shout, the bride takes off her veil and puts on bright honeymoon clothes, the couple goes away to consummate the marriage and the bride is carried over the threshold of a new home.

In Australia I attended a middle-class wedding held in the public gardens of a small town with a state-appointed marriage celebrant instead of a priest. The bride wore a pale pink long dress, her hair covered by a large pink hat; the groom wore a suit with a flower in the button-hole. Rings were exchanged, promises made, and speeches delivered by the celebrant and by the bride's father (who gave her away wearing the national costume of shorts and long socks). There was a feast with cake and champagne, the mother cried and at the end of the party, the couple got into going-away clothes and amidst shouts from the guests, they got into a car covered with grass and shaving cream with tin cans tied to the back bumper bar, and went on their honeymoon. These two young people wanted no empty ritual and no fuss; nevertheless their wedding had all the inevitable elements of a passage rite. The bride was showered into marriage by her female friends and relatives, put on a special dress, received a ring, gave a party, tore herself from a crying mother, changed into clothes amidst clamour and noise, and left in a car covered with a blatant sexual symbol (shaving cream symbolizes sperm) to consummate the marriage. As I write this, two friends of mine who married a week ago are staying in my house; Italians, they shocked their respective parents by marrying in a registry office without the presence of relatives, the bride wore black, the husband refused to wear a ring. There was no ritual as such; nevertheless the basic conditions of a passage rite – separation, transition and reintegration – were present. Relatives later sent presents and congratulations and the two sets of in-laws met and got to know each other. The friends of the couple gave them a surprise party, with spermy champagne and noisy congratulations. Instead of going on a honeymoon, they left the village half a mile away to spend a week in seclusion in the neutral house of a foreigner – me. Their wedding was announced in the local council house. After their 'honeymoon' they will return to normal life as Signore and Signora Nappi.

I believe that passages from adolescence to adulthood, from the unmarried to the married state, from life to death, need ritual, even if the ritual has nothing to do with the church or the pretentious wedding ceremonies of earlier generations. The meaningful marriage ritual can be invented by the couple and their friends, even though abandoning church weddings leads to an impoverishment of cultural symbolism. White Australian weddings should be made more elaborate, particularly because the adolescent-adult passage rite is included with the unmarried-married rite; the ceremony is often over too quickly – 'You put out your cigarette, listen to a word or two from a man in a suit, light your cigarette up again and stand around waiting for the booze while they take the photographs.' Black and White weddings are becoming more and more alike: a few words, a party and off to the beach (White); a few words, a party and off to the bush (Black). The basic conditions of a passage rite are filled, minimally.

The sacraments are being de-christianized all over the western world; do-it-yourself rites are considered more meaningful. Even with the introduction of revolutionary changes in wedding ceremonies Roman Catholics and other denominations are having difficulty making people marry in church. The priest no longer chatters away in Latin; he no longer tells the bride to remain steadfast in her faith and the commandments, true to one marriage bed, 'shunning forbidden embraces and strengthening her weaknesses by firm discipline.' The official guide now reads like a piece from a popular magazine: 'No two love stories are the same. Every couple treads a different path on their way to a love which can form a basis for the life-long partnership of marriage. The wedding service is the time when you openly and publicly proclaim this love which you both have for each other. By choosing your scripture-reading carefully you can tell your friends something about your love story.' Unfortunately the church has not woken up to the fact that passage rites are not founded on 'love'. The *Song of Songs* is suggested as a scripture-reading because it expresses 'the wonder and excitement of physical, sensual togetherness.' Nor has the church woken up to the fact the passage rites are not founded on 'sex'. The guide urges the couple to dispense with formality, to enter the church arm in arm, to recite the vows facing each other or the congregation or with the congregation surrounding the couple. The basic problem is that the church has not woken up to the fact that the significance of the wedding is that it is a passage rite, and as such cannot be a free-for-all.

Widowhood or divorce

Marriages are made, and then marriages are unmade either through death or divorce. Traditionally western women wore white veils when they married and black veils when they were widowed: two different colours for the seclusion period of two important passage rites. Nowadays White Australian widows no longer mourn the death of their masters by covering themselves with weeds, except at the funeral itself; yet the actual mourning period may be prolonged – the widow remains in contact with her late husband by keeping mementoes around her, sometimes even his ashes and occasionally trying to communicate with him through mediums. Black Australians have formal mourning behaviour which helps widows adjust to the loss of one husband and the gaining of a new one. White Australian women do not even move out of the house, her Black sisters move out of the camp; the White women remain resolutely in the matrimonial bed. Nor do they have opportunities for self-expression such as wailing and body mutilation, ritual behaviour which helps Black widows in this time of crisis. Western women, without this stereotyped ritual behaviour, often find it difficult to resign themselves to their loss and many remain grey widows for the rest of their lives, joining their husband in a double grave as they enjoyed him in the double bed. Unlike the Black Australian widow who is automatically remarried to a kinsman of her dead husband, the White widow has no set 'replacement' ready so she must face solitude as well as the loss of a husband.

The burden of mourning for the Black widow is heavy; yet is it heavier than that of the White woman who must bear the loss with stoic imperturbability? The Black widow is smeared with lime or ashes or clay, has her hair cut and may wear a heavy plaster cap on her head until the period of mourning is over. She observes special food taboos and complete silence until released by her new husband. During the funeral she and other female kin are expected to mutilate their bodies and singe off their pubic hair. During the silent period, which may last up to two years, she is expected to behave in a circumspect manner out of respect for her husband's ghost. She communicates with signs, avoids the old camp-site, and is sexually taboo. When the widow's mouth is 'opened', she paints her body with white stripes and sits in the middle of a group of men who hit her with switches of leaves and rub some meal cake on her mouth to 'open' it. She gives a wail and returns to the widow's camp. For a short time, before being taken as a wife again, she is expected to be sexually promiscuous.

People not only get unmarried through death, but through divorce. The undoing of marriage in White Australia is a traumatic passage without rite, without any traditional means to confront a crisis, without ceremonies of transition, separation and reintegration. Why do we refuse ceremonial and even practical help to divorcees when divorce is often a more dangerous crisis period than death, leaving individuals helpless, demented and alone for long periods? Ceremonial and public recognition of the stressful nature of divorce – and death – would help thousands of people adapt to their new status.

The reason for the lack of any ceremony marking divorce in White Australia is not hard to find. Until recently divorce was unacceptable to church and state. All ceremonies concerned with marriage have sprung from the church, and christian culture is unique in its long history of opposition to divorce. In all other societies divorce has been recognized as a way out of a disharmonious marriage. Even in the Old Testament we read (Deut. 24:1): 'When a man hath taken a wife and married her and it comes to pass that she finds no favour in his eyes, because he hath found some uncleanness in her; then let him write her a bill of divorcement and give it in her hand and send her out of his house.' There were means of escaping the permanence of christian marriage – with annulments and formal separations – but until recently only the rich could take advantage of available arrangements even when divorce became legal. Previously, in Australia and America, a couple could not end their marriage without one partner being declared guilty of a legal offence and liable to the cost of the proceedings. Now, with no-guilt and no-blame divorces, the power to pass judgement on the viability of a marriage has been taken out of the hands of the divorce court judge and placed in those of the individuals concerned.

The Australian Family Law Act of 1975 provides a single divorce law for all White Australians. It offers a significant change in the pattern of traditional divorce and separation in the west: it provides only one ground – 'irretrievable breakdown' – for the dissolution of marriage. Proof of misconduct is not required and irretrievable breakdown is considered to be established if the court is satisfied that the couple has lived separately for more than twelve months. About fifteen per cent of all White Australian marriages end in divorce, somewhat lower than the North American rate.

Divorce is part of the normal social life of Black Australians although it is usually the woman rather than the husband who initiates it by eloping with a lover. Twenty years ago, one anthropologist, Elkin, wrote about Black Australian divorce in terms which could equally be applied to White marriage today and which reveal our own ethnocentric christian prejudices: 'The ties between husband and wife are less permanent than we desire them to be in our society; many women become successively the wives of two or more men in the course of their lives; and there are customs of temporary lending and exchange of wives which do not commend themselves to us.'

Divorce in Black society also occurs for political reasons – women change hands between high-status men. Adultery as such is not usually a ground for divorce proceedings, and is rarely the explosive topic it was once with us. Nevertheless if a couple does divorce, the structural situation does not change: the children may remain with the mother but they legally belong to the father's totemic clan; the wife remains in the same 'wife-group' and remarries immediately into the same wife-taking group. When divorce is due to adultery and elopement, the situation is normalized by a formal battle or spear-throwing rite between the ex-husband and the lover. Even if the husband wins he lets the woman go – the fight serves as a symbolic end of the marriage and a sufficiently cathartic means of ceremonializing an awkward separation.

For westerners divorce is not such a straightforward affair. It is an emotional catastrophe symbolizing the break-up of a family, the dispersal of the children and, in general, an admission of failure. Yet there are no ritual or even secular means of helping individuals make this break and adjust to a new status. And it is a new status. It does not entail simply returning to the single state. The passage rite of divorce is unstructured without the beginning, middle and end processes found in marriage and mourning ceremonies. For widows, there are certain customs and behavioural patterns to help them with their grief, but the divorced person, without special clothes or special behaviour is left in a marginal status for an indefinite period, rather like the adolescent without precise initiation ceremonies at puberty. Apart from the occasional divorcee who throws a party or puts an ad in the paper, White Australians quietly accept the social stigma of being divorced and the feelings of guilt, shame and rejection. Here is another moment in a White Australian's life which lacks a passage rite, and which is devoid of direction and ceremonial pattern; the only hope for most divorced people of getting out of the unpleasant transitional state, out of a deviant social category, is to get married again.

It is all very well for a rational government to introduce rational divorce laws. We also need irrational ceremonies to mark the end of marriage and express the new status. Otherwise we are left with easy divorce and psychological turmoil.

Chapter Ten
Sex and Sexuality

White Australians, peeping with curious eyes at the sexual and conjugal habits of their Black neighbours, received the news of Black polygyny, child-marriage, orgies and other unmentionable practices with shocked excitement. White Australian society, a deprived monogamous and frequently agamous population, felt that Black Australian 'regularized sexual unions' (a cold-blooded term used by early anthropologists unwilling to use the christian term 'marriage') involved the marriage of baby girls to senile old men, young boys to old ladies, constant promiscuity and even unions between men and boys. The pornography of early ethnography tititlated in its suggestiveness, in its dashes and euphemisms, its hint at beastly un-christian practices. Unfortunately perhaps for this book, these 'irregularities' — child-marriage, polygyny, institutionalized rape, homosexual unions — lose their scandal value and their weirdness when put in their social place and their proper perspective.

Age
Let us look at 'child-marriage'. Most of us think it immoral for girls to marry at ten or eleven, forgetting that for most Whites through history, the minimum and not unusual age for marriage was twelve not eighteen. We know that Juliet had Romeo in her early teens, that Helen of Troy was married at ten. In Melbourne, Adelaide, Sydney and Perth as well as Dumfries and Miami, the Helens and Juliets of our society are playing with dolls and hockey sticks, hiding their nubility under the nun-like pleats of uniforms and culturally produced juvenility. In most societies, where girls are expected to reproduce as soon as possible, it is the men's rather than the women's social maturity that is delayed.

Black Australian girls, betrothed before they are even

conceived, go to their husbands at puberty, or before, as a matter of course. They marry older men in the knowledge that mature husbands make mature fathers and offer maximum protection for the children as they are growing up. Common sense tells them to accept the situation, and common sense is backed by moral precept and myth. The girl learns from her elders that if she rejects her ugly, old betrothed husband she will be punished; there are poor prospects for a headstrong girl who looks for romantic love and age parity in marriage. The point is that the aunts and myths tell the girl that it is more fun to keep younger men as extramarital sexual partners and husbands as fathers and meat-providers.

In White Australia the ideal of age parity is so strong that any divergences, even by ten years or so, seem grotesque. In western societies today many more people are marrying than they were a hundred years ago and they are marrying younger and younger, to a spouse of roughly the same age; the appalling result is that 'marriage togetherness' now can last fifty years or more. Black Australians rarely experience this Darby and Joan situation. Yet they are not conservative in their approach to marriage: usually the husband is much older, but in some cases the wife may be twenty years older than her husband.

In White Australia the average age of the husband of a woman of twenty is twenty-two or twenty-three; in Black Australia it would be over forty. And the average age of the husband of a woman of sixty is also just over forty. This apparently unusual statistic is explained by the fact that at forty men are at their peak, politically and economically, if not physically; at this age they are able to monopolize most of the wives, young and old. The largest polygynous groups form around young middle-aged men who control hunting resources and ritual information. It is obvious that these marriages are functional and viable, and are not sexual unions between dirty old men and nymphets. A young man of twenty forms an alliance with his future mother-in-law and father-in-law; his wife is born; when he is about thirty, his ten-year-old wife begins to cohabit with him. Anthropologists, unconsciously expecting to find young girls with feelings of victimization, are often surprised when told that the girls like their 'old men'; there is usually a good deal of affection and co-operation between the young women and their older husbands.

In Black Australia romantic love or friendship is not a prerequisite for a happy marriage. The relationship between a husband and wife is not necessarily as close as it is in White Australia where wife and husband are expected to be domestic partners, friends, lovers and totally involved in the nuclear family and household. In Black Australia, as one spouse frequently dies before the other and young girls marry old men, complete dependence of husband and wife is impossible. It is best not to invest much emotional capital in a spouse. Nevertheless there is love and affection between partners who have lived together for years. If a woman falls ill, the husband finds a medical expert and may wander desolate in the bush worrying over the causes of her illness: perhaps a taboo was broken or sorcerer has attacked. His relief is unbounded when she recovers and he watches over her carefully during her convalescence. If she dies the husband mourns and may be greatly upset, declaring himself ready to follow her. Graves are often dignified places made with loving care by the widow or the widower.

Men may seem to have all the advantages: they marry the attractive young girls; they exchange their wives for other men's wives; they are permitted several wives. However the situation occasionally favours the woman. Women change hands several times throughout their lives and while the first husband may be a decrepit elder, the last may be a splendid youth in his early twenties. Old widows are handed over to young men who are waiting for their child-wives to grow up or who may not have found a mother-in-law. Post-menopausal women may not be able to have babies but they are still good yam collectors and sexual partners. The young men marry the older women with alacrity since any wife is better than none. In some cases two youths with widowed mothers may come to an arrangement to 'exchange mothers' in this way. For White Australians the attitudes towards

permanent widowhood and permanent monogamy are inter-
related and the feeling is strong still that widows should not
remarry and certainly should not marry younger men. The
christian notion of one-flesh marriage makes remarriage for
many widows a difficult problem and although the taboos
do not appear on the surface, only a bold woman is prepared
to antagonize her family by marrying in old age a man many
years younger than herself. My own mother was widowed
three times and insisted on marrying for the last time when
she was nearly eighty. I am convinced that few of the hordes
of White widows retired to rest homes and old people's units
would object to the pleasant Black Australian custom of old
ladies marrying their sons' friends. The trend is changing:
already women, instead of living lonely, widowed or divorced lives, form *de facto* marriages and sexual unions with
'boarders' or friends. The old lady who lives in Toorak and
owns a big house, takes in a lodger who cooks, cleans and
shops for her; he, not her son, may inherit the house when
she dies – to the latter's fury and consternation.

A Black Australian girl is, in fact, always married: she is
promised to a man before she is born and she is inherited
by her husband's kin when he dies. Black Australians do
not believe in individual choice as a basis for primary or secondary marriages. Serial marriages now occur in White Australia as well, given the easy divorce laws; a pretty girl or
a determined girl can go through several husbands before
she is thirty-five. Serial marriages for Black women however
are the rule, not the exception. Automatic remarriage after
the death of her husband is often a consolation and a protection for the woman. The brother or heir of the husband is
responsible for the widow and becomes the father of the children; they will already call him 'father' in the classificatory
system of kinship terminology and she will already call him
'husband'. The brother or heir must marry the widow – it
is a duty not a privilege, and wives acquired in that way may
be an economic liability.

Black Australians are classified as 'polygynous' and White
Australians 'monogamous', although the majority of Black
Australian marriages are monogamous, and although White

Australians can marry one spouse after another. I should prefer to forget our ethnocentric habits whereby the majority of people marry a spouse of roughly the same age and go through the various stages of life in tedious togetherness. But, with a married life of forty years and four or five divorces, a wealthy man can be as polygynous as a Black elder. The only problem with this kind of marrying is that the White make-shift system leaves an awful lot of discarded people in its wake. And it gives marriage a temporary feeling which is unique to the west: nowadays, with marriage very definitely no longer forever, despite the ideal and the church, married people seem to be available for remarriage even while still married; some even get engaged to be married to another while they are living with their former spouse. Like the non-monogamous birds and fish, they remain permanently in 'display dress'.

Duties and delights

Another idea perpetrated by ethnographers studying Black culture – and here the blame is mainly Geza Róheim's – is that sex is violent, excessive and really amounts to constant rape of women by men.

A Black Australian girl's introduction to marital sex is occasionally violent. Among certain peoples, the bride is forced to suffer a painful operation which is seen as a symbolic deflowering ceremony before she goes to live with her husband. After her first menstruation, she may undergo an operation on her vagina to signify her marriageable status (see p. 107). Afterwards, the woman's body is decorated with head-bands and tufts made of the tail tips of the rabbit bandicoot, necklaces, arm-bands of fur and her body is painted with a mixture of fat and red ochre. She wears this ceremonial costume as a symbol of her new status and then sends the bands back to the senior man of the deflowering group. She then becomes the exclusive wife of her husband.

Why this symbolic deflowering of a girl who is most probably not a virgin? Black Australians recognize several kinds of sexuality: the sexuality of adolescence and childhood, the sexuality of romantic love and adulterous affairs, and the sexuality of marriage. First sexual intercourse between a husband and his wife is considered a dangerous moment and Black Australians prefer that other, ritually prepared, people perform it. Perhaps the same kind of danger was believed to be present in medieval Europe: with the ceremony of *droit de seigneur* a peasant's lord had the duty – rather than the right or the pleasure – to sleep with the virgin bride prior to her marriage. It is not uncommon for women, especially virgins, to be considered dangerous at marriage and rites attempt to neutralize these dangers. In some places there is merely a taboo on speaking during the wedding night; in ancient Greece the groom dressed as a woman and hid after he had had sex with the bride. In White Australia the groom hides from the bride before the wedding, staying with his mates until the last minute. After marriage he hides the big news from his friends and carries on as if he has not entered the dangerous state of marriage.

Of course what is feared in these cases is not sexual intercourse as such, but the marriage bond as symbolized by sexual intercourse. Whether a bride is a virgin or not, once sex has taken place the couple is united; adultery now takes on a tremendous meaning: the rights of the spouse are infringed and the rights of the husband (and his clan) to the children are usually altered, especially if it is the woman who commits adultery.

It seems therefore that some Black women may be raped once during the normal course of events; White Australian girls are not raped although they may live in mortal fear of it. Yet White women are the ones commonly more afflicted with chronic frigidity, psychosomatic spasms, permanent repulsion from men and male sexuality. Linguistically the words 'have sex', 'marry', 'rape' may be the same in many Black languages. According to some influential observers, such as Róheim, Black Australians form 'one of the few human groups in which the standard form of sexual approach is rape.' It seems that sex is often initiated aggressively by males and an unaccompanied woman on a bush track is as safe as an unaccompanied woman in the back streets of Sydney or New York: fair game for the violent attacks of passing men. In Central Australian sign language, a man with a spear held high signifies: 'I want to marry you'; or 'I want to have sex with you'; or, simply, 'I'm about to rape you'. The typical male attitude is a man holding high the erect spear-phallus, the weapon of aggression; the typical female attitude is a defensive crouching one, hands held ready to protect herself from attack.

Nevertheless it is clear from other accounts of Black sexuality, of love affairs initiated by married women, of adolescent sex, that the standard form of sexual approach cannot be rape. The most common sexual position is rather inimical to the idea of sudden ravishment. The woman lies on the ground and the man squats between her legs, facing her, lifting her thighs on to his hips. In this delicate position he leans forward and steadies his body with his knees. The woman must grip the man tightly around his flanks and buttocks with her legs while he pulls her forward. Another common position is the man on the ground with his legs outstretched while the woman squats on his erect penis – hardly a position for rape. The traditional White Australian position is much more open to aggression and violence on the part of the man. This position, with the man on top of the woman, is rejected by Blacks. It is not only too heavy for the woman, but also a rather bestial, uncultured way of making love and there is always the dreadful danger of mistaking the hole.

Apart from the traumatic initiation into marital sex, the Black Australian girl cannot be said to be constantly in fear of rape. The young Black bride sees sexual intercourse in marriage as one part of the marriage contract. If she is young and her husband unattractive and old, she performs sexually as part of her duties. Young women never complain of the impotency of their old husbands who apparently do not tire of making love; they simply prefer to have their *fun* elsewhere and with younger, unmarried men. Marital sex, reproductive sex is very different from the romantic adulterous affairs. Sex in marriage is a humdrum business. When the girl is handed over to her husband regular sex begins at once; copulating is supposed to make the little girl grow, her pubic hair to flourish, her breasts to swell. Sex with husbands helps form healthy and complete babies in the womb.

Marital sex is a modest, unromantic business and most peoples of the world are cheerful and persistent adulterers. On the whole, marriage is considered a pretty boring affair and the young Black wife, while attending to her duties as wife, mother and in-law, considers it her right to enjoy herself sexually and romantically. A love affair for a woman happily and respectably married to an old man is as essential as a love affair should be to a White wife married to an impotent beer-swiller. Love affairs are initiated by women despite the possible punishments. A double standard as far as adultery is concerned prevails among Blacks as in most societies: an unfaithful wife may be beaten to within an inch of her life and in some cases put to death; her lover is merely ritually speared. The punishment for an unfaithful husband – who already has the advantages of polygyny and wife-lending – is never more than a fierce tongue lashing from his wife.

The spectre of boredom – by confining sex to the marriage bed – is not allowed to haunt marriage. Black Australians seem to agree with Freud that within marriage, a really passionate relationship is impossible. Black Australians spend a lot of time setting up love affairs and enjoying them while they last. The young wife – with the aid of go-betweens, cosmetics, and magical spells made over special food and ornaments – quickly starts a series of extramarital affairs. At the same time men, particularly the young unmarried men, practise love magic to make the women's organs shake with eagerness for them; there is a nice description of a group of Aranda men in the bush singing songs and celebrating sex by making mounds of sand to represent a young girl's sexy buttocks.

The couple makes a secret rendezvous in the bush, usually after dark; the risks are great since the lover could walk into a trap and be speared by a jealous husband. As far as possible the affairs are kept secret; the young man, for example, walks in his mistress's footsteps when they leave camp. Despite the danger, they are rarely caught. Even the girl's mother shuts her eyes to casual romances although she may intervene if a love affair looks like becoming too serious or leading to an elopement. The mother's own interests are involved here: if her daughter leaves her husband, the very special mother-in-law – son-in-law relationship she has maintained for many years, since the ceremony of mother-in-law bestowal, will be cancelled.

Once married, the men are more fortunate than their wives. They may marry two, three, even half a dozen wives. They also have secondary wives to whom they are allowed access in other groups; when travelling a man can satisfy his desires in this way. The boredom inherent in marriage is alleviated by wife-lending and occasional communal sex, activities which are no longer shocking to us in the 1970s as they were to Victorian observers. In Black Australia friends or brothers swap wives in order to enjoy sexual variety; in White Australia wife-swapping is a not uncommon pastime in the great urban sprawl. This revolutionary move has made a hole in the restrictive one-flesh, exclusive concept of christian marriage, and the historical limitation on sexual access to other men's wives and other women's husbands is being breached. The basis of the White system is the same as the Black: the husband uses his wife as a sexual token in a sexual trade. A Black Australian lends his wife to men standing in a special relationship to him; the initiative rests with the husband, as it does in the White case. In White Australia, there is the fear that a wife may compare her husband's sexual competence and be encouraged to seek out extramarital partners on her own like her Black sisters.

In Black Australia sexuality, not marriage, has been ennobled with elaborate preliminaries of courtship, songs and the visual poetry of rituals and ceremonies. Even in the women's rites there are songs with subtle references to lovers, phallic symbols, the emotional aspects of love, the jealousy and possessiveness of romantic lovers. Marital sex is clear-cut and undisturbed by romance and emotion, and thus the old western misconception that Black Australians practised group marriage is hard to understand. 'Group marriage' is a purely hypothetical concept as far as all societies – apart from some types of modern communes – are concerned. Like cannibalism, it is commonly attributed to the conquered and colonialized by the conquerors. Julius Caesar was convinced that the ancient Britons were living in barbaric promiscuity: 'Women,' he wrote, 'are shared between groups often of twelve men, especially between brothers and fathers and sons. But the offspring of these unions are counted as the children of those to whom the maid was conducted first.' Such a misconception of group marriage probably arose from a misunderstanding – on the part of both the Romans and the White Australians – of the classificatory kinship system whereby a man calls his own wife and also her sisters 'wife' and they all call him 'husband'. There is a wife group and a husband group, but the wife's sisters are not necessarily the husband's sexual partners, just as an Australian priest is not a woman's begetter just because she calls him 'father' in the confessional.

In Black Australia sexual outlets from restrictive marriages and enforced celibacy for unmarried men are found in community ceremonies where group sex, as opposed to group marriage, may take place. During the *kunapipi* in Arnhem Land – a festival of song and dance celebrating a cycle of creation myths – there is an element of carnival and sexual partners are freely exchanged. This is a time when secret lovers may meet openly and young men without wives can have sex without fear of reprisals from their elders. These are ceremonial occasions that take place at ritual intervals. In western society today, group sex, performed openly and without taboos, is no longer uncommon among young people. We are living during a time when marriage is lightly abandoned and easily dissolved and when young people are not nervous of copulating in groups. The pornographic ethnography will be written about modern western society, not about the staid, small-scale societies where marriage and the family is still 'sacred'.

Homosexuality

In many ways, the sexual life of a Black woman is longer

and more varied than it is for a man. Girls have sex early and marry early, and immediately seek extramarital adventures. A man's sex life and married life are much shorter; the former is curtailed by unnaturally delayed initiation rites and the latter is often delayed until he is nearly middle-aged. This long period of theoretical celibacy is in fact filled with love affairs which are automatically adulterous since Black women are *always* married. Some affairs are fleeting, others are semi-permanent.

Unmarried men are also permitted sexual union with other men, usually young 'in-laws'. During the initiation rites homosexuality may be practised between elders and novices and particularly between the initiate and the man who circumcises him – his father-in-law or his brother-in-law, that is a member of the group of men who will one day give him a wife. For premarital liaisons, since a cross-cousin or the mother's mother's brother's daughter's daughter is the proper female sexual partner, a cross-cousin who is the mother's mother's brother's daughter's son is the proper homosexual partner. The brother-in-law, in a sense, stands in for his sister. If the mother-in-law delivers a boy instead of a girl, the disappointed fiancé is allowed and even expected to have sex with the boy until he is circumcised. The cousin or brother-in-law is treated in many ways as a betrothed and the 'husband' even carries out the ritual greasing of the 'wife's' or boy-lover's body.

We must remember that Black Australian homosexuality occurs primarily in situations where there are restricted opportunities for normal sexual expression. It is a *faute de mieux* sexuality and accepted as such. In the same way, a husband, during the absence of his wife or during a taboo period after the birth of a child, is allowed 'bestial rights' (as an early ethnographer put it) over her younger brother. Women are permitted – or permit themselves – lesbian relations as long as the partner is a cross-cousin. Girls may use artificial phalluses or merely fondle each other, rubbing clitorises and lying on top of each other. As with male homosexuality, these affairs cease when a girl finds herself a lover. In these situations homosexuality is pleasant and convenient. In other situations, where it is not necessary, homosexuality is vaguely disapproved and classified as 'wrong sex'. Young boys are not told they will go blind or mad, but they are advised to stop or otherwise they may 'weaken themselves'.

Obviously Black Australians have a wider range of permitted sexual response than White Australians, as is the case in most societies where there is no virility problem. Homosexuality is tolerated and recognized as an expressive outlet, serving the covert needs of male and female members of society. White Australian men, at certain periods of their life cycle and also for long weary stretches of their history, have been deprived of women. A frank acceptance of *faute de mieux* homosexuality has never existed in western societies with christian traditions. In Australia, its place has been taken by a very close form of institutionalized friendship known as mateship, a kind of sublimated homosexuality, with strong homoerotic overtones, that grew up when men found themselves isolated from women when they worked in the mines, in the bush or went off to fight in endless wars. Two men bonded together in a relationship which usually lasted until the death of one partner and which provided them with emotional support in a situation where the imbalance of the sexes and social forces operated against normal sex. As a sentimental passion, mateship has provided the theme for countless songs, poems, novels and legends. Today it is part of the White Australian 'Dreaming', elaborated in a rural world which no longer exists, a world symbolized in the male-oriented myth of Ned Kelly.

As we have seen, symbolic homosexual behaviour plays an important part in the Black initiation rites; a homoerotic element is rarely absent from all-male activities whether the all-male groups are German fraternities, African age-grade companions, or groups of White Australian men who drink and play together. A lot of traditional Australian horseplay is symbolic buggery, like the games with the fire mentioned earlier. 'Dating' – sticking a finger between a man's buttocks – is a common joke, and grabbing at another's genitals is considered he-man horseplay. In fact, calling a man a bugger

takes on a special, friendly, matey meaning in some circumstances and given the right tone.

Among groups of Australian men, the veneer of tough
heterosexuality, which we all like to put on, often wears very
thin. In the Arab world, there are transvestite dancers and
whores who provide outlets for the bisexual nature of normal
men. Polynesian villages have special roles for transvestite
homosexuals for the benefit of normal heterosexuals. In the
male strip shows and transvestite reviews in Sydney and
Melbourne, the spectators are made up of 'normal' – heterosexual – White Australian men, along with the odd girl and
'poofter'. When I was in Australia, spending a lot of time
in country hotel bars, I was continually taken aback by the
endless homosexual joking between heterosexual males. I
watched surfies and their semi-humorous gear-dropping. I
noticed that footballers regularly made headline news by
dropping their pants in protest about an umpire's decision.
And how do we explain this news item from christian,
heterosexual Melbourne: two hundred privileged fans were
allowed to shuffle slowly past a rope barrier while their
sports heroes peeled off and took a display shower.

Sexual expression

Black Australians are not perverts, rapists or Lolita lovers.
They happen to enjoy sex in its various forms without any
sign of being grossly over-sexed or imbued with a wildly
passionate nature that can be aroused by the mildest stimu-
lus. We have learned that man has a primitive, instinctive
sexuality that presses for expression. Christians control this
animal pleasure-instinct by culture and taboos; without our
culture and the church, Black Australians, according to the
christian and prejudiced ethnographer, must be animal rapists, Pan-like adulterers and sodomists who go to orgies like
we go to the cinema and swap wives like we swap stamps.

However, as I have tried to show, sex for Black Australians
is not rape, nor is it bestial. It has its prescriptions and
proscriptions, its good manners and poetry. For most of the
time sex is a tame beast as it is for us; few Black people are

prepared to risk everything for the chancy joys of constant
sexual pleasure. Today it is in White, not Black Australia,
that primitive instinctive sexuality is supposedly on the ram-
page in a new, permissive society. The permissive society
for White Australians really means more beer, more
gambling, more pornography: good old-fashioned sex is har-
nessed to advertisements and even political propaganda for
the purpose of selling material goods and future prime ministers.

It is not the Black Australian who is over-sexed, it is the
big White brother who is under-sexed. Real sex is not of
much interest to most people in Australian small towns and
suburbs. Long periods of unnatural celibacy in adolescence
and middle age are accepted with equanimity. Perhaps the
energy is used up in games and drinking: this would explain
an apparently low sexual drive, a drive which declines dramatically after marriage due to boredom, beer, wowser-
wives and a consuming materialism. Moreover, sport is more
important to most White Australian males than are their
wives and children. We have all heard that sex is weakening:
sex and sport, like sex and war, simply do not mix. White
Australians, primitive to the core, require their athletes to
abstain from sexual activities, believing, as did the ancient
Greeks and Romans that as the semen was ejaculated
through the penis, a man's virile strength went with it.
Homer, in the *Odyssey*, wrote: 'Now it is I myself you hold,
enticing into your chamber, to your dangerous bed; to take
my manhood when you have me stripped.'

Black Australians too have their fantasies. Black men have
a preoccupation called by psychologists 'penis captivus'.
They consider rapacious sex with females to be weakening,
and they have a horror about getting stuck and never getting
out. They fear that the woman will grip and hold hard with
the neck of the vagina, almost as though it had teeth, hooking
the rim behind the glans penis and imprisoning her lover-
husband forever.

Our under-sexed White Australian is the inheritor of the
western tradition that holds virginity and chastity as highest
ideals. Marriage, in christian history, has been considered

merely a necessary evil, a concession to weakness and to the necessity to propagate. St Paul's advice to the unmarried and to widows is still heard in the secret soul of most White Australians (I Corinthians 7:7,9): 'I would say that they will do well to remain in the same state as myself, but if they have not the gift of continence let them marry [that means have sex]; better to marry than to feel the heat of passion.'

Black Australians are ardent lovers and they spend a lot of time on sex and its preliminaries. White Australians do not seem to be able to find the time any more for such things as love affairs: time is short and there is much to do, so much money to be made, so much fun to be had, so many things to be bought. The time men spend with their fiancées, their girlfriends, their mistresses and their wives is being constantly reduced; they jump into bed after a busy day at work and following a game of tennis – with any luck and a premature ejaculation, the whole business is over in a few seconds. Sex and loving become subject to time and motion efficiency; copulation is like the quick grill and the frozen food served without ceremony in rapid sittings on uncomfortable chairs: quickly prepared and hardly savoured. People even get married early in order to save time and trouble, and afterwards they remain faithful for the same reason, or from inertia. 'Old-fashioned' prolonged romances, with love magic and songs, flowers and letters, leisurely lunches, need a lot of time – the kind of time the Black Australians have. Sometimes White Australians are forced to have time; the sad statistics after floods, power failure, TV breakdowns, reflect an attitude to sex which is far from romantic.

Black Australians on the other hand have plenty of time for sex, which is given aesthetic expression in love songs, ceremonies, rituals. While I was in Australia, thinking about this book and watching men and women interact, I spent a lot of time by the sea doing 'field work' and incidentally trying to become as physically like the despised Black Australian as possible by relentless sun-bathing. Australians, men and women, go to the beach almost as part of a religious dogma or ideal, finding physical and spiritual catharsis in the sun and the plunge and roll of the great mother sea. Or at least this would be the charitable explanation of the Australian seaside passion which others might explain as an excuse for lazy, burnt-up and burnt-out youth to lie around in the sand, escaping confrontation with life's deeper meanings. Whatever the reason, the beach is a ceremonial ground and surfing a passionate rite with thousands of followers who play the eternal sun–sand–surf syndrome. Surfing – a Polynesian rite associated with sex and gambling – was imported to the West Coast of America and Australia where it took on different meanings, although it is still a kind of ritual.

Like so much ritual, serious surfing effectively excludes women. One day on the beach, I was distracted from my reading by the splendid bodies of the surfers floating out to sea, their blond hair bright on their shoulders. In front of me their women sat patiently on the sand in tidy feminine circles. While the beautiful men glided casually out among the sharks, the girls made useless eyes at them from the edge of the sea. Instead of searching each other's heads for lice and ticks or removing worms and thorns from their feet, the White Australian women rubbed each other with sun-tan oil, combed each other's hair and picked off pieces of peeling skin: the beach is an in-between place for Australians, between the sacred sea and the profane land, a rare place where they can be natural and indulge in grooming and body contact.

As the men met the waves and rode them in a glorious moment of temporary suicide, speeding through the spray to the groups of humble women, I was reminded of the Black Australians. In one totemic ceremony performed by initiated men, the women remain on the edge of the sacred ground, watching the dances and listening to the myths. The women rock together to the music, beating their pudenda with their hands in time to the movements of the men. The men move with a quivering or trembling motion which causes the white down of their body decoration to shake off; the down floats in the breeze over the heads of the men, as the spray of the surf seems to hang over the heads of the surfers. As the down leaves the Black men's bodies, it is transformed into immaterial particles; as it settles on the women sitting in huddled groups, it is thought to enter their bodies as part of the long process of spiritual and physical procreation.

Although a surfboard is cared for like a sacred object and in many ways becomes part of its owner's personality, although it is polished and painted, nobody has thought of attributing phallic or coital symbolism to the boards and their role in the surf. My aim in making this easy comparison is not to prove that Australian surfing is a meaningful sacred rite; I wish it were. I only want to indicate briefly the beauty of the symbolism of Black Australian sexuality in contrast to the fleeting superficiality of one of Australia's national sports.

Part Six
Passage to Death

Chapter Eleven
Growing Old

Growing old, like growing up, is a gradual process: there is no precise moment when a westerner can say that he is an adult, or that he is old. In some parts of the world, adulthood is associated with the birth of a male child; then the parent begins slowly dying as his child or children take his place. White Australians may get the vote at eighteen and be pensioned off at sixty-five, but maturity and middle age and old age are not clear-cut cycles associated with physiological or cultural stages. In fact youth is being stretched unnaturally to accommodate the aspirations of old men of forty and fifty; we have invented vague categories such as 'young middle-aged' to reassure those growing old that they are still young. In the same way, we have 'invented' testosterone and oestrogen and the upper-middle and middle-lower-middle classes. 'Young middle-aged' in most societies would be just plain 'old'. When Byron died at thirty-six in 1824, after a full – to say the least – life he was not 'young middle-aged'. He was old and had already attained the average life expectancy of adult men of that period.

In Black Australia, the average life expectancy is probably the same as in eighteenth-century England. Two hundred years later in the west, life expectancy has risen to an amazing age: about seventy for men and seventy-five for women. This revolutionary change has led to the formation of 'old cultures' in the west, with an ever-increasing population of 'elder citizens' living with kin, alone, in special communities or travelling hopefully-hopelessly around in caravans and ocean liners. Their children, their *old* children, imbued with the mystique of youth, forever 'young' thanks to sun-tans and make-up, look at the increasing number of old people and shiver – seeing no beauty, no usefulness in them. For fun-loving people like White Australians, the sight of the old conjures up a spectre of death and its inevitability. So the old are hidden as far away as possible in old people's homes and ghettos. For their part, the old are no longer prepared to sit in a rocking chair and knit or to play the useful and once-admired roles of grandmothers, grandfathers, aunties and uncles; they too try to escape their low status and the scarcely concealed distaste of the young by assuming young roles and a determined independence.

Old age has its physical signs: we lose our hair, our oestrogen and our testosterone. Westerners are forcibly retired from work at an arbitrary age. Yet we refuse to celebrate the passages that take us out of one age category and into the next, thinking that the passage rites can only celebrate a progress towards a despised condition. So we maintain that we are only as old as we feel – or at least as old as our friends and relatives and our pockets let us appear to be. In contemporary Australia and North America, 'old' is a dirty word when applied to human beings – not to dogs and bric-a-brac; from its first physical signs – loose flesh, menopause, flagging sexual appetites – we begin masquerading as juvenile ancients. In most cases we succeed admirably, simply by combing the thinning hair forward, dyeing it, flouncing it, pulling in our tummies and buttocks, smartening up the breasts and adopting the bright clothes and the bright smile of youth. Not for us the little satisfactions of old age: the benign smile, the relaxed, spread body, the greys and blacks of suitable clothes. When in Europe, my mother startled the sombre widows with her bright new teeth and hair, her youthful carriage, her cheerful, young ways. Eighty? Impossible. Married three times? Wonderful. And myself. Forty-odd, in young jeans with a slim figure, carefully dyed in the right places by the Mediterranean sun. Forty? Impossible. So much energy and so fond of young people. Wonderful! Of course Italians are very polite. Despite the efforts they make, old White Australians are still old and the sensations of the physiological process of ageing are felt by all of us, Black and White alike. Drugs, and artificial aids and attitudes are only of limited help in disguising the facts.

Ceremonies of maturity and old age might help. Marriage

may serve as a passage rite into adult status, but from that moment on White Australians are not content to exploit their increasing years; they see them only as the numerical sign of physical and social decline. Once a woman married and her husband called her the 'old lady' and her children called her 'mum'; now they all call her Joanie. Once children called their father 'old man' and left him more or less to himself and his age-mates. Now he often likes to be called by his christian name, even by his grandchildren; he wears the same kind of clothes as they do and plays as good a game of tennis as he ever did.

In other parts of the world old age is not feared, it is celebrated. The older you get, the more you display the fact by letting your grey hair and flaccid breasts hang out. In Africa, the menopause is a prestigious status change for women and often celebrated; the non-reproductive woman takes a more important part in community politics and rituals. In Mali, people have a ceremony which celebrates longevity; special prerogatives are given to men and women who have attended two of these great rites which are held only every sixty years. The really great people are those who have attended three, which means they must be at least one hundred and twenty years old!

Senility

On the other hand, while most societies give respect to the old – because of their control of property, sacred knowledge or simply because they have survived – there is a universally ambivalent attitude to the old, especially to the very old. Senile people are considered abnormal, even dangerous; when they lose their power to do things or to control themselves and others, they lose their power to command respect. Old women, particularly widows, have always been prone to witchcraft accusations. In all societies, old people do have a niche: they sit still in special chairs in special corners, they should wear special 'old' clothes, eat special 'old' foods and not interfere too much in the business of the community. Their sexuality, like that of the very young, must be sublimated and repressed. In Europe at one time, remarriage of

the old met disapproving or mocking reactions; the couple
had to endure a cruel cacophony raised by the young who
felt that sex was their prerogative. In France it was called
'charivari' and in England the serenade of pots and pans was
known as 'rough music'. In Italy today a widow or widower
would be risking the same kind of abuse if he or she attempts
to marry in a village church. When my mother married at
eighty, people in the small town where she lived certainly
did not give their unqualified approval.

Respect for parents, grandparents and the old in general
is one of the aspects of Black Australian community life
which is frequently praised by early observers. There is compensation in being old – old, not senile. The woman as grandmother or senior wife continues her role as a protective and
succouring maternal figure. The man, as he gets older,
acquires greater knowledge of the totemic myths and
becomes learned and powerful and is treated with respect,
even reverence. 'Old age' however is a relative matter; in
Black Australia men in their late forties and fifties monopolize most of the women, ritual information and economic advantages. Ceremonial deference, particularly from younger
relatives and 'sons-in-law', is paid to them for these reasons.
They are formally embraced at public gatherings: the
younger man falls on his knees and rubs the old man's
stomach with his forehead. The Black Australian says that
tribute is paid to these men partly because they have successfully escaped the common dangers of a very perilous way
of life and partly because they have accumulated wisdom
which they, and only they, can pass on to the younger generation.

Nevertheless Black Australians also have ambivalent attitudes to the very old. A man who reaches sixty-odd becomes
known as a 'grey-haired old man', and his advantages
become less and less tangible until he has only ritual prerogatives. Finally he doesn't even have these. Senility approaches,
creating problems for Blacks as well as Whites. When they
reach this stage Black Australians become more 'nuisances'
than 'venerated old relatives'; in most Black Australian communities the name for the old during this helpless period

is, in pidgin English, 'close-up dead'. The hunters and gatherers living in nomadic communities now expect the 'close-up dead' to get on with dying. Very old age, therefore, has few advantages for the individual or the group and the senile are treated as socially dead. While old age in general may be said to be a process less accompanied by anxiety and loneliness than in western societies, there comes the moment when the survival of the community depends on the death of the 'close-up dead'.

For a hunting community the problems of old age are obviously greater than for a settled urban group. The old are treated with love and respect but once they are unable to provide for themselves or accompany their relatives on essential hunting trips, they may have to be left behind. For weeks or months the old will be treated with special kindness, receiving their share of food and being carried for miles on foraging trips. Eventually, although there is no established practice of doing away with the aged and infirm as such, they may be put away. The Tasmanians had a kind of euthanasia: they left the old or the very ill person in a hollow tree or under a ledge of rock with sufficient food for a certain period; the old person either recovered and survived or didn't. This behaviour is no more heartless given the circumstances than depositing an old relative in an old people's home or leaving him alone for months on end in a service flat. For the Tasmanians, euthanasia was a fact of life since the nomadic hunters had to be on the move in order to survive.

Nowadays White Australians, like North Americans, are mobile to the point of nomadism; but it cannot be said that they have to move in order to survive. Yet we leave old people to look after themselves or leave them, virtually deserted, in private and public 'homes'; we now talk nicely, in a civilized way, of voluntary euthanasia. Old age in White Australia is a nuisance. Old people become obsolescent like old cars. They are not guardians of mythical knowledge; they do not possess the majority of sexually mature young women. They are of no practical or spiritual use and therefore become socially dead even before the Black Australian who

is left in a tree trunk. They are forcibly retired into uselessness at the age of sixty or sixty-five. They have been per-
suaded by their children and the government to sign away
their hard-earned property to avoid death duties. In doing
so they have also signed away the respect and love of their
children. Death duties were originally planned to redistrib-
ute unearned wealth, but the practical result has been that
parents hand over their money and their estates long before
they die; although a pragmatic approach to material matters,
the practice can leave them high and dry in a community
that depends on a continual exchange of wealth and on social
interdependence. Old White Australians are of little value
once they become poor. They are also of little value as spiritual or social guardians, storytellers, even gardeners or baby-
sitters. Early retirement and the early transfer of wealth kills
them socially so that their physical death twenty years later
is merely an inconvenient, embarrassing and guilt-laden
afterthought.

Are there any solutions? First of all I suspect old people
should initiate an 'Old People's Liberation Movement'. The
old should be forcibly moved out of their spiritual and physical ghettos and back into the world. They should also be
encouraged to take a more serious view of life rather than
spending the long years of retirement thinking only about
fun and tours and clothes – selfish pursuits not at all restricted to irresponsible youth. Such 'fun' though may also be
a celebration of the end of their responsibilities.

A new *vieillesse dorée*? Part of that renaissance must include
a ritual celebration of old age. Since the status of the old
is low in White Australia, most people avoid the clothes and
other symbols of old age. The Black Australian on the other
hand makes a feature of his balding head, for it is seen as
a sign of maturity. He also scarifies his body with signs that
indicate his progress towards respected old age. A lined face
is ugly because we have been taught to think so. Retirement
is pathetic because we have not been taught to think otherwise. The menopause is a time of distress because our culture

has decided that it is a sign of decline and is simply an opening to a long, miserable path to death.

Menopause

With the menopause, women have a clear physical sign of the onset of middle age, and it is a process that only the human female among the primates of the world appears to experience. The changes of the menopause are physical changes even if they are less positive indication of a life crisis than the menarche. The breasts change – the fat decreases and glandular tissue is replaced by cordular material. There are also changes in the external gentialia and the internal reproductive organs. There is a gradual regression and atrophy of these organs which return to the conditions of a pre-adolescent girl. The lips of the vagina become smaller and thinner and the vaginal fold disappears. The main change of course, and the one marked by ceremony in some societies, is that women no longer menstruate.

Other females in other primate groups – the baboons, the macaques, the chimpanzees – continue to give birth regularly until death. The menopause, therefore, is a very human problem: we have nothing to learn from animals. Most societies, including Black Australia, accept it as a step forward into a new kind of life, an important positive change. Moreover, although there is not much information in anthropological literature, it would appear that the menopause in most societies is unaccompanied by the distressing physical and mental symptoms that White women suffer. African women and Black Australian women look forward to the period of relative freedom: freedom from incessant childbirth, freedom from the taboos associated with childbirth and menstruation. Old age is valued and the woman who enters it continues in her role as protector, healer and affectionate companion of the young. Black Australians are given a new name and new prerogatives, including the right to see more of the sacred ceremonies. In Africa, post-menopausal women lose many of the disadvantages associated with sexually dangerous (that is reproductive) womanhood. They become 'men':

they are allowed to join men's secret societies and enter sacred precincts forbidden fertile women. It is after the menopause that women enter the public sphere, taking part in village politics and village rituals.

Western women enjoy none of these immediate advantages of their menopausal state. While their Black sisters enter a new phase of the life cycle, the White women go through the mental agonies of the menopause, as they went through the agonies of puberty. Some of them struggle to remain little sexy girls for their husbands and new boyfriends, disguising the facts of physical change, denying old age. Of course, for a White Australian woman the menopause is a prelude to many years of active life and therefore has a greater significance for them than for the Black Australian woman whose life span is statistically almost over when she reaches this phase. Perhaps for this reason western women refuse to treat the menopause as an occasion for a passage rite; rather it is considered part of a simple gradual process of ageing, a kind of illness, a deficiency state due to the loss of hormones which can be replaced artificially.

I think this is a mistake. It means that another phase of the natural life cycle passes without public recognition, without ceremonial attention. Menopause, like other physical phases – beginning with the menarche – is basically a taboo subject , and its manifestations, at least until recently, have been private concerns and considered pyschotic, not to be made public or ritualized. During the uncomfortable years of the menopause, there is no traditional symbolic behaviour to help a woman pass from physical youth into physical old age. Without this ceremonialization unpleasant physical and nervous symptoms may flourish unnecessarily as they do during the uncertain period of puberty. While about half of the women in White Australia pass through this period with no side-effects whatsoever, the other half are victims of a dramatic ordeal which includes hot and cold flushes, dizziness, long periods of depression, unreasonable promiscuity, even nervous breakdowns. It is during the 'change of life' (the linguistic term expresses perfectly the revolution that occurs at this time) that the incidence of suicide among women is higher than at any other period in their life cycle.

In many ways, the symptoms of an unsuccessful passage from youth to old age are similar to pimples at puberty, excessive morning sickness and food fancies during pregnancy, and tooth excision of thirteen year old adolescents. A woman becomes a victim of current myths which define her only in terms of her role as fertile biological organism. When she ceases to menstruate, she feels she is a failure, ugly, useless. She may delude herself that she is becoming more masculine, that she is sexually insatiable or that her sexuality is withering away. While it is clear that certain physical changes are indicative of the ageing process, there is no reason why a woman should feel that she has no further merit. There are no precise scientific causes for severe physical incapacity or exaggerated psychological reactions; but even if there were, it seems that the environmental, cultural situation precipitates these periods of stress at puberty and the menopause. The problem is that a woman no longer has a determined role: she is not a willing grandmother; she is not a wanted mother-in-law; she is not a source of traditional knowledge and folklore in the community.

Menopausal symptoms are symbolic manifestations of a life crisis with which we can not come to terms. Just as Black Australian men share their pregnant wives' food taboos and morning sickness, White Australian men are now being encouraged to feel menopausal symptoms in their forties and fifties. Although unable to experience the traumatic physical changes of the menopause – they will go on being fertile, if less potent sexually – many husbands are accompanying their wives through a period of transition from youth to old age, sympathetically experiencing depression and the occasional dizzy spell in exactly the same way as Black Australian men experience labour pains. Although in the 1970s, only nine in every thousand – or some such unreal statistic – are the sad victims of the male menopause, the numbers are sure to increase as the word gets round. Men who suffer certain physical symptoms of a general and natural physical decline are given honoured treatment as menopausal subjects. The menopausal male is physically no longer a youth, yet he combs his thin, greying hair forward, goes to the gym and courts younger and younger girls. Others descend with their wives into depression, suspicion and hypersensitivity. For a woman, the situation is worse because the cultural opportunities for symbolic expression are greater. Bored in the confined space of a suburban home, lavishing her creative energies on the lounge-room curtains and chocolate layer-cakes, she has no exigencies of work or family role to help her grow old gracefully. She may give herself up to drinking, gambling or sex, ridiculous hobbies and women's clubs; cosmetics and fashion.

The problem of the menopause is not a problem of hormones: it is the problem of accepting the approach of old age, the facts of grey hair and paunchy stomachs. The main problem is, that like adolescents who have no means of coping with sexual maturity, the middle-aged have no rites and ceremonies to help them into a mature and contented and positive old age.

Can society take an original step such as introducing rituals to celebrate the beginning of old age? Few societies have taken very elaborate note of the menopause, either because it has little cultural significance or simply because, like the apes, women are already dead before it happens. However since we are now living twice as long as we used to, it would seem logical to give public recognition to the physical facts of ageing. The psychotic symptoms might disappear if the change were dressed up in symbolic form and given signposts as are other social changes. A uniform? An entirely new job? Some women throw a party to celebrate their liberation from the bonds of fertile sexuality (but not sexuality of course). Others take on more work at the local Red Cross or run a jam stall for the Guide Dogs. Others join local discussion groups and read Robert Ardrey's latest book; or play bowls dressed like district nurses. In my opinion this is not enough.

Retirement

Maturity, or old age, should be celebrated early – not when the state decides that a man or woman is no longer fit for work and pensions the worker off. At eighteen, the child becomes an adult. At sixty or sixty-five he or she is declared obsolescent, pensionable and unproductive – sent back to childhood. The individual is given no choice between work or no work, just as the Black Australian youth cannot choose between circumcision or no circumcision. Westerners are compelled to retire into social death, but are not reborn. The rules were laid down a hundred years ago when high mortality meant that life expectancy was nearer forty than seventy and only individuals with special luck and strength survived into old age. Australian society plans systematically to retire men and woman into a world of sweated leisure, after a lifetime of work; often they have scarcely enough financial resources to make the remaining years dignified or comfortable.

As a passage rite retirement is a pathetic step into old age. A ritual handshake from the boss, a ritual clock and a ritual drink symbolize not a beginning of anything new, but only the end of forty years of work; it is a crisis rite celebrating the transition from adult usefulness into old obsolescence. The sixty-five-year-old says good-bye to his workmates, and as part of the formal rite of separation, hands over to a younger person on the workbench. He frequently smartens himself up for the final ceremony hastily carried out during the lunch-break or in a hotel bar after work. During the relaxed period of the ritual, the group laughs and jokes and the bosses let their hair down a little and are unusually friendly. The retired man then takes his cheque and his presents home to his wife and settles down to domestic emptiness.

This period of retirement, the passage from work to leisure, from mature adulthood into old age, has all the symptoms of another crisis and *nearly* all the elements of a classic status passage: group celebration, transition, the exchange of gifts, special drinks. However, the ceremony, unlike most passage rites, does not accentuate the move into a new life except insofar as the worker is separated from his mates and his place of work. There is no rite which incorporates the central figure into a new age-grade – the community of the old, the retired, the pensioned-off. Perhaps a formal ceremony into retirement would be adding insult to injury since the only status most workers get is that of the useless old man, a status marked by stigma rather than prestige. You can't have rituals to induct a man of sixty-five into a functionless interregnum.

What is needed is a new approach to old age. Earlier retirement followed by a new occupation, perhaps, during the difficult 'menopausal' period when the children are leaving home and a new lease of life is appropriate. A woman is better off in a way. If she survives the menopause in her forties and fifties she probably will have already accumulated a number of cultural activities: hobbies, clubs, groups of friends. In the small Tasmanian town where my family lives, with a population of less than three thousand, my sister counted seventy-three clubs and associations, most of which served the interests of women. A man however has devoted his life to his job and perhaps a few sports and other activities usually suited to young men. At retirement he leaves the public world and is thrown into a domestic world to which he is unaccustomed, a world dominated by women and children. Unlike the initiated Black adolescent who is ritually separated from the world of women and children, the retired worker is forced back into it. And for the majority of White Australian 'mums' who have never worked, the idea of having 'dad' at home is an irksome one. Queen of the home, she will make it clear that the 'old man' is more of a nuisance· than a companion and will certainly not give up her morning coffee with the girls, her afternoon bridge with the girls, her nature walks with the girls, in order to keep her husband occupied. She will expect him to potter around in the fowl-house and the vegetable patch. He may prefer to sit in an armchair in the sunroom and give up, unless he has maintained contact with his mates and the all-male culture of the pub and R.S.L.

At sixty-five, the White Australian statistically faces ten years or more without working, ten years with nothing to do. As Carl Jung prophetically wrote: 'Completely unprepared, we enter the afternoon of our life; even worse, we

do it under the wrong assumption that all our former ideals
and beliefs still hold. We cannot live the afternoon of our
life using the same programme we had in the morning.'

We need ceremonies and preoccupations to mark the
approach of old age. But not the ceremonies and preoccupations that go with the young-as-you-feel syndrome. Black
Australians are concerned about the onset of old age and
its accompanying physical degeneration; they all worry
about their health and the men, their potency. They do not,
however, worry about their looks, and as for smartening up
their old bodies with paint and cosmetics, their attitude
would be the same as that of an old African woman who
said to me, 'Why bother? Who wants to call attention to an
old body?'

At the menopause, when the Black woman is reconciling
herself to a quiet but not an empty life, her White sisters
are undergoing cosmetic surgery, attempting suicide, joining
Weight Watchers, decking themselves out in youthful frills
and painting their faces like fertile nubile girls. White Australians try to retain youth and attractiveness by magical
medicines and diets which are supposed to take as many
years off 'old age' as they take kilos off bodies. An entire
industry is devoted to cosmetics claiming to contain female
sex hormones which supposedly give adolescent femininity
to the menopausal figure.

Why are there no rituals for old age? Unfortunately the
west has so glorified the distinctiveness of being young and
the seductive qualities of youth that any ritual passage out
of this mythical state must be problematic. In Black as well
as White Australia, youth is special: the most beautiful
people, the most sexually attractive, are girls who have just
reached puberty or the newly initiated, circumcised young
men. No middle-aged Black Australians, however, would
attempt to imitate beautiful teenagers. Middle-aged White
Australians are determined to remain in the youth culture,
rather than to enter a period of middle-aged tranquillity.
Dress, styles of speech, the kind of car bought, the food eaten
and the cigarettes smoked, are chosen to help us appear
young, at least to our coevals, if not to the young themselves.

Instead of giving up active sports, bright clothes and cosmetics, westerners are hypersensitive to the signs of old age: out of breath at tennis, wrinkles on the face and fat on the bum are all 'stigmata' of decline and furiously camouflaged.

This obsession with youthful looks and youthful attitudes means that old age when it comes, comes as a shock. White Australians have upset all the natural phases or stages of age. A modern woman is never middle-aged and never – heaven forbid – old. The kind of mature, full-blown womanliness, which has always been part of a middle-aged woman's attraction in all societies, has been masked by artifice and gymnastics. Until a girl is about sixteen, her jealous mother tries to camouflage her as a baby girl. Once out of the mother's clutches, the girl dresses as a young woman and tries to remain a young woman until late in life. At sixty, although she may not know it, an Australian or American matron is bedecked as a maiden with all the signs of a sexually available teenager.

Of course I admire the cheerful, young approach and the fitness of Australian couples in the seventies and eighties who take to the long desert roads and the international tours. But I am not convinced that fat pensions and face-lifts are an adequate answer for the problems of the old. Pensions are spent and face-lifts are shaded in the hot sunshine of Australia's California, the irresponsible funland of the Gold Coast of northern New South Wales amd Queensland. In cases like these, I think White Australians could take a leaf out of the Black Australian's book of life by growing up sooner, getting old quicker and taking less time to die.

Chapter Twelve
Dying

Taking less time to die? Harsh words for people who have learned to face the facts of life but not the facts of death. If we are going to come to terms with ageing, we shall also have to come to grips with death. Westerners, in deciding to get younger and younger, by hook or by crook, and to get another drop of fun out of life, have pushed death into the penumbra of tabooed untouchability. Once upon a time sex was the ogre, now it is death: instead of being frightened of fucking we are frightened of dying. We used to be taught that sexual frustration made us neurotic and aggressive; I believe that an exaggerated fear of death and a refusal to accept and celebrate it is making us neurotic and aggressive, and from a young age. We are now taught that a continuous sex life into old age keeps us fresh-skinned and bright-eyed at ninety; I believe that instead of learning to have a guilt-free sex life without a sudden seizure, we should be preparing for approaching death.

Euphemisms for 'fucking' were once more common than now, but we also have euphemisms for dying. Children were once kept clear of the sexual aspects of life, and told that the stork brought babies. Now we watch films on television of babies being born. Death, on the other hand, remains shameful and indecent and is no longer given a public viewing.

Funerals and mourning
I spent more than twenty years in Australia without seeing a corpse or attending a funeral. When my distant relatives died, there was some whispering in the lounge; cards and flowers were sent, but innocent children were not expected to attend funerals. When my father died, I did not even put on a crepe band and I never carried flowers to his tomb. It

certainly did not occur to my mother to put on widow's weeds or to cover herself with lime or mud or tear out her hair as a respectable Black Australian widow would do to show that she has suitably honoured and mourned the dead. Yet death is the last status passage and an important one, at least for the people left behind. Instead of wild public demonstrations of grief, feigned or unfeigned, we are left with a vague mist of guilt. My mother, when her second husband died – my father – was left with guilt and a difficult problem: as she had thoughtlessly arranged for a double grave for each husband – a kind of marble doublebed – she had to decide which one she would get into. Characteristically, she solved this problem by marrying again.

White Australians have hidden death away; many of us are able to push the deaths of our nearest and dearest far into the deep pool of our unconscious. This attitude, we must realize, is unique in ethnography. Almost universally, the living are used to death; they are brought to the death beds of dying people; they are taught the facts of death. We are taught only the facts of life, and when grandfather dies, the grandchildren are often told he was taken away in a car full of flowers.

I have witnessed death at close quarters only outside Australia. I then learned that the customs in Australia are decidedly exotic: a notice in the newspaper, a black-edged mourning card, a funeral, sweep out the room and back to normal. For ten years I have lived in an Italian village of a thousand people; the whole community takes part in death from the moment of dying, through the tolling of the death knell, the visit to the corpse, the public burial. In Africa, a great wooden drum is beaten in the market, and from the special rhythms chosen by the drummer, the people far and wide know whether a child or an adult, a woman or a man, a commoner or a chief has died. They all stop what they are doing and traipse to the dead person's house to view the corpse, to talk of the illness and death, its natural and supernatural causes and comfort the close kin of the dead person.

In Africa, my own difficulties in dealing with death were revealed by my usual fainting spell. Frightened of the idea of death, I first tried to avoid burials and funerals, autopsies and corpse-watching, but my professional ambition demanded that I conquer this dread. The first couple of times, I passed out alongside the corpse, once half inside a freshly dug grave. Everyone was amazed at my own 'dying', as fainting is called in Bangwa, but again I was accredited with an amazing sensibility to the presence of the spirits. Gradually I grew accustomed to people dying and learned the importance of death celebrations, keening, elaborate mourning, and the participation of members of the community in the intimate facts of dying.

Death is as important a status passage as birth, and one which is ignored at the community's peril. Although death is obviously an important stage in the life cycle of the dead person, its effects on the lives and statuses of the people left behind are even more important. The community loses a member, a wife becomes a widow, children become orphans; the dead man rejoins the world of the spirits in some way, even in our agnostic society. The grief of the community, publicly expressed, finds expression in socially accepted ways. It is unnatural to express grief only in private. Some people wail and sob endlessly. Others gash their bodies with knives and lop off fingers and toes. Victorian widows covered themselves with 'weeds' and hid behind black veils. Africans cover themselves in mud and sing dirges.

In the eighteenth book of the Iliad, Achilles mourns Patroclus his friend:

With both hands he rent the black mould from the forced earth
    and poured it on his head,
Smeared all his lovely face, his weeds (divinely fashioned)
All filed and mangl'd, himself he threw upon the shore,
Lay as laid out for funeral, then tumbl'd round and tore his
    gracious curls.

Achilles' behaviour is typical of normal mourning behaviour in ancient Greece. I had always thought this description was of an extreme case of half-crazed grief for a specially loved friend. In White Australia, this important passage rite has been stripped of essentials and thoroughly messed up. The living make token gestures to the dead and then carry on as if nothing has happened. They look embarrassed when a funeral passes, try to avoid the bereaved and bear their grief stoically and alone. Why they don't even have a party any more – funerals once included a gathering of mourners at which special meats were served.

In Africa my friends tore their hair and covered their bodies with 'black mould' just like Achilles. They wailed and wept ostentatiously and sang dirges in honour of the dead person. A few months after the burial, they dug up the skull which is kept as a memorial; and they did in fact have wonderful parties, with dancing, feasting and singing, to celebrate the death of their father, mother, child or friend. Homer's description can also be applied almost phrase by phrase to the mourning ceremonies of Black Australians who 'rend the black mould from the forced earth and pour it on their heads', wail like crazed beings, throw themselves on the ground and 'tumble around and tear their gracious curls'. The only trouble is that the anthropologist's description is less than poetic: Black Australians 'cover themselves with mud' and 'tear out their hair' and 'cut off their fingers'.

In reading about Black Australians' mourning customs it is difficult, but essential, for a White Australian to realize that their customs are much more 'normal' than his own. In most societies, the pattern is similar: a person dies, there are expressions of personal and public grief, the natural and supernatural causes of death are ascertained, the body is washed, decorated and sometimes mutilated, it is publicly displayed, publicly celebrated and then disposed of. Usually the family or even the whole community moves away from the dangerous or polluting scene of death; the dead person's name may become taboo and personal possessions may be destroyed or buried. Rites and ceremonies and mourning may go on for months and even years; there is usually a second funeral when the community celebrates the life of the dead person and performs rites designed to speed the spirit away from the land of the living to the land of the dead.

Funerals, more than weddings or initiation rites, benefit the community, the living left behind. Stereotyped behav-

iour during mourning periods attempts to control and channel personal grief by providing standard ritual expression.
The rituals allow the expression of a dreadful sense of loss
and deprivation on the part of close relatives and the community; they also control the inevitable feelings of guilt and
self-accusation that accompany the death of a close member
of the family or friend.

This guilt is minimal if the person who dies is old, has
lived a full life and was prepared for death. For this reason
death ceremonies vary in their degree of pomp and celebration according to the status of the dead person, his age
and what relatives and property he has left behind. Both
Black and White Australian societies make certain differen-
tiations. Stillborn babies, unwanted babies, criminals and
suicides are buried or cremated without fuss. Black Australian infants, who have been named and incorporated into
the community, are mourned intensely by their mothers and
family members when they die but there are usually no
important community ceremonies, no inquests into the
supernatural causes of death and relatives make no move
to avenge their death. Infant mortality rates are so high that
death in childhood is almost a normal fact of life and the
mothers and close relatives *must* try and forget the child ever
existed.

On the other hand, mature adult males of middle age have
elaborate, spectacular funerals. Again women are buried
with less fuss than men in both societies and the very old
have simple rites. My mother's first husband died as a young
man, the father of four young children and his memory is
still celebrated in the family and the community. Her second
husband died when he was over eighty and more or less
senile: his funeral was a simple affair and he has no public
memorial. My sister's baby who died a few days after birth
and my brother's child who died at a few months were sin-
cerely mourned in the nuclear families but they were buried
quietly and the facts of their life and death are no longer
mentioned or even known. Yet mementoes of my sister, dead
at ten, are found all over the place.

Although my own attitudes to death and corpses are

particularly immature – so that even now I resist going to a funeral or even visiting hospitals – it is some comfort to know that corpses and death *are* considered fearful things by most societies. To go to a funeral makes everyone realize that his own body is subject to death and decomposition. White Australians whisk the corpse off to funeral 'parlours' where it is coolly laid out by strangers, who are not affected by its polluting nature. In other cultures, the corpse is kept at home and is embalmed, painted or dressed up in an effort to create an illusion that when the body is put in a box or a sack or on the top of a platform in the desert, it will endure in its basic physical form and not rot. I was once given the place of honour at a funeral and found myself sitting next to an elaborately bedecked corpse which looked hardly more dead than the venerable chief on the other side. Associated with this idea of the alive-corpse is the belief that the body must be transformed, through the correct manipulation of symbols and rituals, into a ghost or a soul or an ancestor who lives in a heaven or some other kind of other-world. Bodies rot and bodies become dust. Funerals and mourning behaviour purify the society of all that is unthinkable and chaotic about the death of a member of the group and all that is unthinkable and chaotic about a rotting corpse.

Still, White Australians do treat death as a passage rite, even if the dying man has expressed a wish to be buried 'without fuss'. Briefly the traditional procedure is as follows: a few close friends and kin gather around the death-bed to take part in a ceremony which a priest or minister conducts, commending and sanctifying the soul of the dying as it passes from this life to the next. (Nowadays this aspect of the passage rite is often ignored.) Next the friends and family are joined in a burial or burning rite by members of the general community – poor men and women usually have the smallest processions. The social expression of death sometimes consists of a special meal or the wearing of mourning clothes; once, the widow was semi-secluded for a certain period and forbidden to marry for a number of years and she would never marry her husband's brother, who is exactly the person the Black Australian widow is obliged to marry. These cultural expressions of the community's loss and family grief are gradually being abandoned. A White widow may wear pink the day after the funeral and she will certainly not accept restrictions on whom or when she should remarry.

Our tentative, nervous approach to dying and death must be compared unfavourably with the intensely involved attitudes of other peoples. In Africa, the sick-bed is surrounded by a crowd of concerned relatives and friends; when I lay 'dying', I barred the door and prepared to go it alone. When a Black Australian lies dying, his relatives gather around, chanting and crying; his wives may compose a lament. Close kin crouch over the dying man in turn and rub their chest against his, then lie on top of him. While the men turn their backs and hide their faces, the women approach the sick man and clasp him. These actions help the dying man come to terms with death, help him lose, or at least loosen, his tenacious grip on life, help him 'take less time to die'.

As soon as he dies, an announcement is made and leafy branches are piled over his body. After the mourners throw themselves on the body or mutilate their own – the initial demonstration of grief – they cover themselves with special paint or mud, each colour indicating the relationship of the mourner to the dead man. Wailing continues in the camp the night following the death. Once again the body is used symbolically in the passage rite: a fingertip is chopped off as an expression of grief; the wailing women cut their heads with digging sticks and the men make gashes in their shoulders and thighs. Blood flowing is a sign of mourning, like wailing. They are violent but satisfying expressions of grief which have been tabooed from our own restrained rites.

When the elaborate process of mourning is over, the body is disposed of by exposure, cremation or burial. This final ceremony can be just as elaborate as the mourning ritual. In the northern parts of Australia, the body is exposed in trees before burial, while in the south it is buried immediately; cremation apparently occurred in Tasmania. In the first case, the corpse is carried into the bush by specific relatives who find a tree and build a rough platform about ten feet above the ground. The hair is cut from the corpse and kept by a senior relative; in some cases it was customary for relatives to eat some fat or meat from the body as a sacramental sign of the loss they have suffered. The female relatives sit at a distance waiting for a smoke signal to indicate that the body has been successfully exposed: they then begin loud lamentations and again mutilate their bodies. A day or two afterwards, the widows are painted with their husband's totemic sign and their long and tedious period of mourning begins: they cease to wail and are bound to a vow of silence for months or even a year. The corpse is left in the tree for a time until the bones are cleaned by sun, wind and scavengers; the bones may be then smeared with red ochre and buried or put in a hollow log and burned.

Mortuary rites, burials, corpse exposure, mutilation, accusations of sorcery, wailing, widows' mud and weeds, embalming, cannibalistic sacraments are all part of the important passage rite of death for Black Australians. Each ritual deals with the universally shocking fact that a live person has become dead meat and each aims to separate the spirit from the corpse and speed it on its way to a new resting place, preferably a long way away from the survivors. As in all passage rites, Black and White rituals concerning death involve three stages – separation, transition and reincorporation. The dead man is separated from the living: in White Australia the corpse is quickly bundled out of the house, the furniture is rearranged, the body is buried in an open space away from houses. Nowadays, the cemetery is not much more than a garden where lawn soon covers the insignificant hump and the dead are really 'buried and gone' after a few weeks or months of desultory flower-bringing. Black Australians treat the dead with more respect. The ritual separation involves the fumigation of the corpse, breaking its bones, stopping up the orifices, burning the belongings and moving camp. There is a taboo on mentioning the dead person's name, at least until it may be safely assumed that the spirit has departed this life for ever. This taboo is extended to all words which sound like the dead person's name; they are dropped from the vocabulary and other words invented in their place.

The second phase in the rite, transition, is carried out by disposing of the body through cremation, exposure, mummification, even necrophagy. During this stage, the death should be noticed by the whole community and talked about. The mourners discuss the death, the dead man, the way he died, and receive commiseration from their friends and in-laws to whom the story of the illness or accident should be related in detail once again. In White Australia, one of the worst aspects of the 'flight from death' is that mourning is becoming the business of the people intimately concerned and no one else, not even the next-door neighbour. Very often even close relatives allow the hospital, the funeral parlour, the crematorium and the church to deal with all aspects of death. During the time when they have to deal with death, widows, mothers who have lost children – the living – find they have no close friends and relatives to turn to for consolation and help: kin and neighbours excuse themselves from intimate commiseration by maintaining that death is a private sorrow, a personal matter. It is nothing of the kind! Death is an event that concerns the community, and the close relatives and friends of a dead person are able to survive the crisis only by exhibiting their grief publicly, weeping in the arms of friends and talking, talking about the death, and about the dead person. Most societies have learned that one of the immediate needs of the bereaved is to talk: to talk about what happened before the person died, what happened immediately afterwards, what the weather was like, what the doctor did and what the ambulance man said. They need to repeat the details over and over again. This talking is part of the passage rite. It reveals a need for sympathy and is a personal expiation of the guilt feelings which are commonly associated with death.

The crisis of death must be made public. In White Australia, the family and neighbours are informed and a notice put in the paper. In Italy, printed notices are pasted on the town walls. In Black Australia, as soon as someone dies, the wailing begins: it is really loud so as to satisfy the neighbours and the dead man himself. A member of the camp is sent to others in the area to tell the news and a long-distance runner is sent off to distant communities to inform important relatives. The spreading of the news of death, like the spreading of the news of birth, shows that critical passages cannot be kept private. Death is of public concern and even passers-by show respect when a hearse passes. In small-scale societies, of course, death is much more of a public calamity than in industrial and urban communities; ceremonies may last for months and the whole village or the whole clan is expected to take part. Even in the west it is almost impossible to die privately – in secret – since even if you request no flowers, no funeral service, no fuss, the requests are rarely acceded to: the funeral is not for the dead but for the living – it channels the disturbed emotions of the survivors into meaningful and cathartic expression. Moreover death is public because it usually involves the exchange of goods, the distribution of the dead man's property to his kin and friends.

Natural and supernatural

Anthropologists point out that there are natural and supernatural causes of death for Black Australians: that is, a man may die from a snake bite or yaws but some other thing – sorcery or witchcraft – must have caused the snake to bite that man or that illness to carry him off. However, death is both natural and supernatural for us as well. When White Australian widows and fathers talk about the dead person, about what they did, and said, what they wished they had or had not done, they are expressing their belief that death is not a simple straightforward physiological process. In talking over and over again about the death, in blaming themselves, in remembering unimportant incidents which occurred during the illness, the bereaved are exhibiting behaviour similar to that of the kin of a dead Black Australian who seeks to discover the sorcerer who brought about the death. In Africa it is believed that the dead will not rest in peace until the supernatural attack has been traced. In White Australia, without sorcery and witchcraft beliefs, the priest in the confessional, community advisers and psychoanalysts step in to help settle the disturbed, guilty minds of the bereaved and help them bury the dead once and for all.

Black Australians attempt to divine the causes of the death by examining the state of the corpse on the exposure platform – the pattern of the body's exudations, or of the holes which form in the earth above the grave, the appearance of the internal organs, are the clues. Only the death of a very young child or a very old man or woman is considered natural. An old person dies, he is mourned and he is buried: death is timely and death is his due. In Central Australia an old man is buried in a shallow, unmarked grave; the hair is spun and brought back to the camp; mourning is not elaborate and the death is not expiated.

The death of a young person, or a man or woman in the prime of life, cannot occur naturally. Death is attributed to the effects of witchcraft and some time after the death all the relatives of the dead person assemble and carry out an inquest. The elders ponder the signs, an expert draws their attention to a special mark or a strange noise. They come to a decision, taking into account current feuds and quarrels, past adulteries and elopements and steps are taken to punish the sorcerer.

Once the culprit is identified, certain patterned ritual behaviour follows. The pointing bone is a well-known Black Australian example of supernatural punishment. A visible missile is transferred to the body of the sorcerer causing his death. I will not go into the details of how Black Australians succeed in carrying out incorporeal-corporal punishment since the details are always vague, second-hand and unsatisfactory. However, it is clear that through an erosion of self-confidence, an accused man may be convinced of his guilt and co-operate in his own destruction. Aware of the sorcery, of the bone pointing at him, he may begin to notice a slight headache; he gives it importance, worries about it, until it becomes worse, finally insupportable. The man feels hunted, becomes suspicious of everyone and everything and there are outbursts of temper against the people around him. He finds it difficult to eat and refuses help from his relatives and true friends. As a result of this psychosomatic behaviour he becomes ill indeed and sometimes dies. I have witnessed this process in Africa where witchcraft accusations cause neurosis, fear, illness and death, often by suicide. None of this behaviour would be difficult to understand in the atmosphere of suspicion and doubt of witchcraft accusation. It occurred in medieval Europe, and in western countries today many psychosomatic illnesses, often fatal ones, have only supernatural causes.

In 1965, in Canada, for example, a healthy woman went through a minor operation and regained consciousness after a successful outcome. The following morning she had a relapse and despite every effort made by the doctors she died. Post mortem examinations revealed an extensive haemorrhage mainly of the adrenal glands without any other explanatory pathology. It was then discovered that she had been told by a fortune-teller that she would die at the age of forty-three. She had had her forty-third birthday the week before the operation and she had told her sister that she was going into hospital to die. Black Australians are mocked for their superstitious beliefs, yet millions of westerners are flocking to the fortune-tellers, astrologers and the purveyors of exotic religions.

A belief in sorcery and witchcraft, apart from the individual tragedies involved, in some ways is a more satisfactory solution to feelings of guilt about death than individual emotions which have no ritual outlet. Witchcraft and sorcery direct emotions and aggression outwards; personal feelings of guilt direct it poisonously inwards. Sorcery, along with formal mourning patterns, weeping, condolence cards are a means of helping the survivors come to terms with the nasty facts of death. Death must not be ignored: it must be imbued with symbolic and emotional meaning. Death is a shocking event to Black and White Australians alike, a shock to close relatives and a shock to the community; things have to be put right through the ceremonial of a passage so that mourners may be slowly reincorporated as normal members of society.

Spirits of the dead

In most societies to die is not to be annulled as a person, but to accede through funeral rites to a new status, to achieve the formal status of 'the dead', to become an ancestor, a ghost or a totemic spirit once the necessary passage rites are completed. White Australians traditionally went to heaven, hell or purgatory or limbo; nowadays many claim that they go nowhere and that they do not want a permanent existence in another world. Black Australians return to their spirit world, a world closely involved with that of the living since the dead man may be reincarnated. The spirit is considered indestructible and the human personality splits into various totemic parts which return to their individual spirit homes. Some people believe that these spirits and bits of spirits wander near the community for a while after death, and that the complex funeral rites help drive them off to the relevant totemic world. Without a proper funeral, the spirit may remain behind and worry the community like our ghosts; or people who died wrongfully may wander around like Hamlet's father's ghost to torment the survivors.

Christian funerals have supportive social functions; but they also serve to appease the dead man and the ghost of the dead man is sent away from the living by various rites. Just as flowers were once held at the waist to ward off the plague, so the flowers accompanying the corpse and those put on the grave are thought to ward off the dangerous spirit of the dead. The Black Australian belief that the ghost of the dead remains in the vicinity of the community for a time is parallelled in White Australia: the bereaved continue to take flowers to the grave, stopping only when the spirit has moved on out of harm's way.

Death is a true status passage; rites and ceremonies convert a corpse into a totemic spirit or an ancestor. For christians, the last sacraments, extreme unction and the other rituals of death emphasize the passage from life to death of the dying person, and only secondarily do they convert the dead person into a spirit or a ghost. Black Australian ceremonies aim to provide the dead person with an appropriate state after his death. Today White Australians are not very interested in having a social status after death; the corpse is disposed of in an unfriendly and prosaic manner, sometimes with the minimum of ceremony. Death is becoming less and less a passage rite, less and less a social event; a once shocking event is being denuded of its emotional meaning. Death has little meaning for rational White Australians except as an untidy and tedious reminder of its inevitability.

Conclusion

The need for ritual is a human universal and in all societies, rites and their symbols have functions which vary from the level of etiquette to that of deep religious significance. The sign of the cross may help an old lady cross a busy street. Grace gets us into the right mood for a communal meal. We have seen that rituals may accompany a shift from one status to another or confirm the privileges of superior groups in society. Ritual may be aesthetic or 'fun'. 'Ritual symbols' said Aristotle of the Greek mysteries, 'are treasured for their own sakes and there is always a great aesthetic pleasure in taking part in a rite.' The rites of passage discussed in this book, ostensibly concerned with individual maturation, also serve community needs.

At a funeral, the main actor may seem to be the corpse, but in fact the rites are for the survivors. The ceremonies convert the dead man into a ghost or an ancestor, and help assuage the grief of the people left behind, channel aggression and encourage group and family cohesion. Baptisms and weddings require the presence not only of the principal actors, but also of their parents and relatives and friends. A passage rite is normally a prerequisite for membership of the social group, and members of the community take part as a sign that the community will continue and that individuals will not become isolated from it. When social links are weak or being weakened consciously by the state, couples get married alone, grow old alone and individuals die alone. Rites of passage are social events and can only have meaning when other people are present. Fortunately, even in our cold bureaucratic society, as long as there are some friends around, a group of neighbours, an aunt or two, some kind of ritual performance is usually forced on the parents of a new baby or newly married couple. Ritual binds together friends and relatives and neighbours and sustains the sense of identity of the local group.

The importance for the individual is perhaps paramount. Ceremonies at life's crisis points, like chapels besides rivers to be crossed, help people cope with natural fears. Rites make an individual aware of the significance of a new behaviour pattern: a young man becomes a husband, a husband becomes a father and his personality is adjusted accordingly. There is no doubt that the physical and social passages are accompanied by emotional changes which give rise to personal tensions, feelings of inadequacy at marriage, guilt at death, fear of the unknown at puberty and menopause. These tensions and fears can be minimized by ritual because the change is accomplished with public knowledge and approval. They can also be minimized by the cathartic nature of many passage rites.

Ritual serves important psychological functions: the emotions of grief, fear, even anger are released at funerals, initiation rites and marriage. Puberty, menopause and old age are traumatic crises and the emotions are best expressed and discharged through symbolic behaviour. Verbal confessions to priests, psychoanalysts and close friends offer only a very incomplete catharsis of these feelings. The current fascination with violence, horror and disaster in television, fiction and film may reflect the need for release, but such vicarious relief can only be temporary and superficial.

Black Australians accept the facts of emotional distress and provide formal release in dramatic initiation rites and funerals. Western society has bottled up emotion and blocked its dramatic expression. At funerals mourners should be allowed to luxuriate in grief and allow the stages of the ceremony to resolve these violent emotions, through catharsis, into a state of acceptance. Greek drama was concerned with universal human anguish and alleviated it through intense emotional expressions. The guerilla theatre of communist China also offers individual and community catharsis: the suffering of the peasants over the centuries is evoked in plays that elicit mass weeping and shouting; the political denouement at the end is the satisfactory resolution.

Rituals, therefore, can help individuals and the community by allaying tensions and calming irrational fears. For this reason alone, the western trend to ignore the most striking and impressionable periods of life risks both private and community peace of mind.

Ritual also has more subtle functions; like etiquette, it serves as a magical mediator on a great number of social occasions. In Africa I found myself learning complex ceremonies of greeting and farewell and there were rites before and after eating. In Italy the mini-passages of everyday life are oiled by mini-rites: greetings are made before buying food or getting on a bus; although people may not always say grace before eating, wishing everyone *buon appetito* is *de rigeur*. In Australia you can do the week's shopping without greeting anyone; we may even enter a roomful of friends without saying hello and leave without saying good-bye. Most people find that etiquette helps in everyday passages, in the transition from one social situation to another. Meeting people and leaving people are accompanied by ceremonial phrases that indicate the entry into a new relationship or the difficult nature of separation. Grace before meals helps in the passage from one behavioural pattern to the next and temporarily binds together individuals who, away from the community table, have separate interests and activities. The religious meaning of the words of the grace may have no importance as countless good little White Australians know. One lunch time the members of a Cambridge college were completely oblivious to the fact that instead of the usual Latin grace the rhyme 'eeny, meeny, miny mo' had settled the community into the mood for a successful meal. When I was a child, prayers helped me make the fearful passage from day-time to night-time, but the words of the spell I uttered had as much religious meaning as a prayer in Sanskrit.

Philosophers since Aristotle have been postulating on the basic difference between us and the animals. Humans need, for some reason, to believe themselves unique in the animal world. Once the gift of language was considered the unique trait; but linguists have shown that non-human primates can communicate by signs. Then it was incest taboos: but ethnologists have shown that non-human primates tend to avoid close relatives as sexual partners. Boswell defined man as a 'cooking animal': 'The beasts have memory, judgement, and all the faculties and passions of our mind, in a certain degree; but no beast is a cook.'

My own definition of *homo sapiens* might be that he has passage rites. Now that many of us are giving up incest taboos, and fire and cooking, and even losing the gift of articulate speech, we need to hang on to the ceremonies of birth, death and marriage. The life cycles of all animals, of course, include the basic stages from conception to death – prenatal life, infancy, youth, maturity and old age. But no animal as far as I know has learned to mark off these periods by ceremony and rite. Animals and some westerners do not become circumcised at puberty, get married and have funerals. Animals of course do have 'rituals': a bird holds a stem of grass in its beak and woos a female and then throws away the grass; we know such activity is derived from nest-building movements. But this is automatic behaviour, like our habits of eating, washing, love-making. Ritual must be a conscious symbolic statement about social behaviour. Ritual is not the regular meal, but the grace before the meal; not the habitual bowel movement at eight-thirty but the prayer before the bowel movement; not going to bed at ten, but the prayer before going to bed.

Passage rites help the individual mature, help him define the reality of his new status, help him feel that he has really changed, that he has become a different person. Among Black Australians, we have seen that the transition periods from childhood to infancy, infancy to adolescence, adolescence to adulthood take place in a series of well-marked ritual jumps. White Australians and all westerners no longer have a traditional model for these status changes. We advance as individuals, slowly and with a great personal struggle. Black Australians have a rigid model for transition from immaturity to maturity; they perform the great dramas of their culture for the benefit of adolescents and display their art in religious cults; the universal themes of life are communicated in symbols and religious images in their dances and ceremonies. The symbolic patterns are on the mind of the initiate: they have the force to change the infant-androgyne into a sexually mature man, a man into a husband, a husband into a father. I doubt that White Australians ever mature satisfactorily – they suffer life-long immaturity because they are without this symbolic imprinting. At puberty, for example, I filled myself with food, put salt on my pubic hair, pined away with excessive masturbation. Might it not have been better if my elders and betters had rounded me and my age-mates up and told us in no uncertain terms that the pervasive sense of sexual excitement, the physical changes, meant that we were ready to start living as men?

Black Australians have symbolic behaviour involving cultural taboos, avoidances, passage rites, and formal etiquette which contribute to a sense of community belonging and of individual maturity. My suspicion is that we White Australians do not grow up at all. Once upon a time it suited westerners to consider primitives child-like creatures who lived for the moment; the boot, it seems to me, should be on the other foot. A constant theme in the nineteenth century and not so nineteenth century was that Black Australians exhibited the behaviour of uninhibited and impulsive infants. Yet the actual accounts of their individual sense of responsibility and cultural achievements seem to contradict this prejudice. Spencer and Gillen, the most influential of early reporters and the foremost theorists of the 'child-like nature of the aborigines', frequently gave themselves away. Watching Black Australians who were studying the complex symbolic performance of a ritual involving the churinga stones, they commented that 'the sustained interest was very remarkable when it is taken into account that mentally the Australian native is merely a child, who acts, as a general rule, on the spur of the moment.'

After a very short time in White Australia in the 1970s, an observer would probably conclude that the present White inhabitants of the continent are incapable of sustaining an interest in philosophical and theological problems like those involved in sacred churinga knowledge. And it would take him less time to amass enough evidence to prove the infantile behaviour of this far-flung example of the civilized White race.

Yet, we White Australians do not see our food habits and our colourful language, for example, as part of a general immaturity associated with the lack of meaningful passage rites. They are part of our attitude to life that converts everything into fun and games. We are a drinking, sun-loving, water-splashing, nut-brown people living in a child's paradise. Australia, like America, is the place for the young at heart and the fun-lover, where life is spiced with the fantasies of faraway islands and unlimited sensuous pleasure. Food and sex, exploited in advertisements, reflect our wish to play forever.

I do not think my claim exaggerated when I suggest that Australians do not grow up because they do not have celebratory ritual at times of life's crises. They do not grow up because there are no means for them to do so. Once marriage and parenthood were stepping stones to responsible adulthood in White as well as Black Australia; then followed comfortable middle age, grand-parenthood and the gentle decline into old age. All these statuses are now well and truly despised by a fair proportion of White Australians, as is the ritual that traditionally accompanied them. We confidently believe that we are a secular people with no need for ceremonial and ritual. Yet people run around inventing patriotic ceremonies, national anthems and Australian flags. While the 'reasonable' young mock church christenings and weddings, few of us are free from irrational beliefs, medical placebos, unreasonable hopes or from faith in the power of luck, from the old tags and the new taboos – from magical behaviour in fact.

Western thinkers have long maintained that there is an essential difference between magic and religion; usually behind this arbitrary distinction lies the conviction that 'we' have religion and 'they' have magic. Anthropologists have recently challenged this dichotomy, and it is now clear that westerners are not the only ones who have rational, logical and scientific ideas and 'primitives' are not the only ones who believe in magic and myths. The French writer, Lévi-Bruhl, wrote that in the mentality of the primitive nothing is what it appears to be: everything serves as a symbol of something beyond the real world, and is an image pointing to a magical reality. Even westerners must realize that nothing is merely what it seems to be: a single object – a motor car or an advertisement – may have an infinite range of associations that have little to do with science or objectivity. Despite its rationality, western society has never succeeded in fostering a sense of complete objectivity.

If there is a distinction between magical thought and rational thought it is not one between two cultures: it is the difference between two aspects of one culture. Every society needs the rational and the irrational; magical behaviour simply reflects universal human fears and weaknesses and the need to call for strength from the outside. In christianity magic has an important place: we light a candle to St Anthony to help us find a lost object; a St Christopher medal helps Protestants and non-believers to avoid accidents. The old belief of Catholics that if they eat meat on Friday they come out in spots is a magical belief. The efficacy of the sacraments and of the doctrines of incarnation and resurrection depends on their primitive, magical powers. No religion, however high, however low, can make a satisfactory break between magical and religious behaviour: Black Australian beliefs, the ancient Greek mysteries, Buddhism, Hinduism all have a religious core shading off into magical beliefs. The recent reforms toward 'rationality' within the Roman Catholic church are in error precisely because of the failure to accept the validity of magical behaviour within all religions. Friday abstinence, the Latin mass, the mystery of the Eucharist had magical meaning though no rationality.

Rational life needs the prop of ritual, magical action, the use of visual and physical symbols to epitomize the important realities of life. Superstitious beliefs and practices are deeply rooted in our unconscious mental processes. To be rational in a life which is patently unreasonable is asking too much of human beings. It is for this reason that we should not deny the critical events of life a ritual elaboration. We may avoid the idiosyncratic inanities of the psychoanalyst's couch and the superficial salvation of ephemeral religious cults if we mark these important moments appropriately. The danger is that, without strict guidelines, our attempts to override life's perilous passages may result in a rash of illogical, neurotic behaviour. In the early eighteenth century Defoe, in *Journal of the Plague Year*, described a similar situation: 'These terrors and apprehensions of the people led them into a thousand weak, foolish and wicked things, which there wanted not a sort of people, really wicked, to encourage them to; and this running about to fortune-tellers, cunning men and astrologers, to know their fortune, or, as it is vulgarly expressed, to have their fortunes told them, their nativities calculated, and the like, and this folly presently made the town swarm with a wicked generation of Pretenders to Magick.'

The situation is hardly different in Australia, north America and Europe where religion is being abandoned in favour of the myriad forms of psychotherapy and cults. In times of doubt and uncertainty, people try sex therapy, marital therapy, family therapy, behavioural, existential, primal, gestalt and radical therapy and seek to be treated by thousands of Pretenders to Magic: Freudians, Jungians, Adlerians, Hornevians and Reichians. You can try yoga, shiatzu, acupuncture – all can do wonders for your indigestion, your sexual vigour and your peace of mind. The religion of millions of westerners has become trivialized into obsessions with health food and with the state of their bodies. Food is dressed up as myth, quacks as priests, the aspro as a magical symbol. Black Australians follow their bodies and their souls through a great symbolic dialectic while White Australians scream drunkenly after Mickey Mouse on a float or a popstar in a Rolls Royce. Imagining themselves rational products of the industrial revolution, they are falling into a wild chaos of superstition and they have replaced belief in god and the efficacy of magical ritual with food taboos, pet totems and comic book figures.

Black Australians, on the other hand, are deeply religious people, with their faith evident in every aspect of their life and being. Initiation rites dignify man through religious drama and symbols; a pregnant woman expresses her changing state by not eating certain tabooed food; the community respects sacred objects; the group looks after the sick and the bodies of the dead are religiously prepared for an afterlife. We are not dignified by religious drama and symbols. We grow unnaturally fat and pimply at puberty instead of undergoing meaningful initiation rites; we get married in five minutes at a registry office; a woman at forty-eight can insist on having a hysterectomy although the doctor finds no medical reasons for it.

There is real danger that we have lost the ritual habit. We have been taught by misguided psychologists and sociologists that we can find salvation through reason or through sex. Prophets have decried irrational behaviour, empty ritual, wasteful celebrations. People have been told to deal with personal crises on their own, to grapple with insuperable problems. We quickly, but individually, realize it is an impossible task and in the dark moments of doubt and inadequacy we realize we have no formal behaviour to hang on to.

Most of the critical periods of life are still looked after by the christian church, and rites at birth and marriage and death are carried out by priests and ministers in churches. Once the Roman Catholic church fitted the christian sacraments to the major crises of an individual's life: he was born into the church through baptism; he was confirmed; he participated in the rite of the holy eucharist; he was given the sacrament of penance if he sinned; his marriage was hallowed and made permanent by christian rites; and when he died a priest administered extreme unction. The church understood the profound human need for ritual support in moments of crisis.

Today, although the great symbols of christianity have lost their force and the central core of the christian message has been forgotten by the majority of people, the church still provides opportunities for celebrating births, marriages and deaths. No longer do people believe in heaven and hell; no one is compelled to go to church on Sundays, or to read the bible or the sacred myths. Yet while giving up christianity, people in capitalist Australia and communist areas of Italy where I live are still taking their babies to be christened, their fiancées to be married and their dead to be buried – in church. In White Australia, although less than ten per cent of the population go to church regularly or even begin to understand the basic ideas behind christianity, more than three quarters still christen their children, more than half marry in church and over ninety per cent are buried by a minister of the church. Non-christians celebrate these rites in church partly because of their respect for tradition, partly because it is difficult indeed to invent new rituals.

The interesting thing is that the persistence of the rites betrays a deep need in the human psyche for rituals to accompany the biological rhythms of life. Some people maintain that there is no real necessity to have the children baptized if the parents are not practising christians. Why marry in a church at all? The state provides all the opportunities legally necessary to name a child or register a marriage, but it does not provide ceremony and ritual. The state is attempting to take over from the church and also the family: it ratifies marriages, protects children, supports fatherless and motherless families, confirms broken marriages, decides about the age of marriage, the education of children. However the state cannot provide the 'magic' of a religious passage rite.

On a different level, the state is trying to take advantage of human beings' need for ceremony and ritual by incorporating religious feelings into apparently secular ceremonies. National ceremonies and symbols are invented to dress up the meagre content of bureaucracy, democracy and communism. The Chinese communists have successfully created national ceremonies which are really religious rites. The Russians have their May Day parades. The communist party in Italy is challenging the church by arranging elaborate celebrations to compete with local saints' days.

In Australia, one of the few ceremonies celebrated throughout the nation is Anzac Day, the Australian memorial day. The myth of Anzac is derived from Australia's contribution to two world wars; a piece of history has become a sacred myth, a religious model for human action. In imitating the mythical acts of sacrificed heroes, the White Australian detaches himself through rite and symbol and enters the 'dreaming', magically, in exactly the same way as a Black Australian re-enters the sacred time of his dream during the totemic rites. The point is that Anzac Day is a religious ceremony in celebration of the state. The sacrifice of Australian youth at war provides a collective catharsis and suffering for the whole nation and elicits much more religious fervour from the community than any christian ceremony.

If we can 'invent' such a satisfying religious rite as Anzac Day, a rite dedicated to the memory of the country's martyrs and celebrating virility and fertility, why can't we invent similarly powerful rites for the benefit of individuals? Anzac Day ceremonies and Memorial Day rites in America are potent political symbols which use religious feelings and symbols for the benefit of the wider community. They teach that ultimate wisdom, morality and happiness reside in the constitution and the head of state. The state 'knows' that rituals create a rhythm for public life and can be invented. Without national ceremonies, flags, anthems, uniforms, the state falls apart.

Without structured behaviour, particularly at critical periods of life, people too, fall apart. Adolescents, widowers, divorcees, mentruating women, retired workers, menopausal males and females are forced to suffer the stresses and strains of life's passages without the comfort of ritual and community recognition. It is during these crises that individuals are most vulnerable: psychosomatic illnesses, suicide attempts, depression increase dramatically during these periods. Yet we are offered nothing more than the shabby makeshift solutions of welfare agencies, psychoanalysis and drugs, social workers and drink. It might well be possible to avoid serious psychological disturbance at these times by having public ceremonies with the individual or the group of individuals concerned as the centrepiece.

The sanity of the community depends on the sanity of the individuals. If something goes wrong in converting a child into a sexually active adult, a single woman into a married woman, a man into a father, a fertile woman into a post-menopausal woman, the whole community will feel it. The individual's need for a satisfactory symbolic life is as important as the political ceremonies, the football matches, the television programmes provided by the modern monolithic state. Yet the state may prefer to house a population of de-ritualized, desymbolized dehumanized cyphers whose personal crises are managed by national health programmes, insurance companies, massive community parades, subsidized tranquillizers and condoms. But if individual lives become dominated by the superstate and passage rites are replaced by a kind of mass hypnotism, we may have to renounce forever any hope of a sane transition from childhood to old age and death, and accept the tragic distortion of the human psyche and universal moral immaturity as the lot of modern man.